M000073579

THE FIRST-TIME MOM'S POTTY-TRAINING HANDBOOK

THE FIRST-TIME MOM'S

POTTY TRAINING HANDBOOK

A STEP-BY-STEP GUIDE
for Success
at Every Stage

MEGAN PIERSON, MA

Illustrations by Amy Blackwell

ROCKRIDGE
PRESS

This book is dedicated to you, mamas! Being a first-time mom can be challenging and isolating, but also fills your heart with joy. I see you and I hear you. Keep putting one foot in front of the other. You go, Mama!

Contents

Introduction

Welcome to the wonderful ride of POTTY TRAINING. Potty training is like hopping on a roller coaster. The ride is long, there are lots of twists and turns, you don't know what to expect, and you may get wet. Some people say it's great, while others leave running. This is exactly the way I felt with my first child. I was excited, scared, nervous, and not sure what I was getting myself into.

I am so glad you're here. Just the thought of potty training can be scary and unnerving. Potty training is not ever taught in school, so how are moms supposed to just know how to dive into it? What are the ins and outs of potty training? What are you supposed to do step-by-step during this process? How do you go into potty training your child feeling confident? This book is here to provide you with practical tips, tools, and explanations, as well as advice to inspire, encourage, and equip you with the best knowledge to successfully potty train your child.

Twelve years ago, my first child was two, and the moms in my local moms' group were talking about potty training their kids. They had different ideas on how to potty train and had read lots of different books on the subject. I got anxious thinking I should also potty train my sweet firstborn. So I bought some books that really confused me (one told me to make my daughter run laps around the house when she had an accident). Eventually I decided to just dive in without ever role-playing with her, letting her explore with a small potty, talking to her about potty training, or even really thinking the whole process through.

I thought, *How hard can this be? I have a master's in early childhood special education, I can do this.* WRONG. It was a nightmare. Like, a *serious* nightmare. She cried, I cried, we cried together. I would stare at her while she sat on the potty. I would repeatedly ask her if she had to go potty. I set a timer ... and she ended up with a UTI. See? I told you it was awful! Finally, my pediatrician gave me the best advice: "Megan, take all pressure off of her and just let her have fun with the potty for a while. Then, dive back in when you are both calm and ready."

I promise you that your first experience potty training your child will NOT be like mine. As a potty-training consultant and toddler specialist, I have spent the last 12 years researching, meeting with pediatricians and urologists, talking with moms all around the globe, writing a potty-training manual, and consulting on potty training. I have potty trained my own three children, dozens of my friends' children, and thousands of children around the world. You are in good hands. I have done the research, so you don't have to spend the time doing it. My goal is to support and guide you through this journey. I promise to give you the skills you need to feel confident potty training your child. Potty training is something you will do *with* your child and not *to* your child. It can, and should, be a bonding experience. Although I can't promise you will never feel frustrated, I can guarantee that if you stay calm, consistent, and positive, you will get through this together. *The First-Time Mom's Potty-Training Handbook* will equip you with the skills to successfully tackle potty training, taking you from readiness to success.

PART 1

An Introduction to Potty Training

Two of the main questions surrounding potty training are: How do you know when your child is ready? and What steps can you take to prepare? Talking about readiness is not only for your child—it's also for parents. We will take an in-depth look at the readiness signs and how to start potty training when you, your child, and family are in a "high tide." We will also look at common potty-training myths so you can figure out what's fact or fiction.

Every child is different, so looking at your child and their personality will guide your decisions. You will also need a good tool kit to stay positive, consistent, and ready to tackle any challenge that comes your way.

Potty Training as a First-Time Mom

Let's dive in. This first chapter will help you feel confident during the potty-training process. We'll look at signs of readiness and learn that every child is different and will approach potty training differently.

Welcome to the Wild World of Potty Training

This is an exciting time for both you and your child. Potty training is one of your child's first chances to show independence and take pride in their accomplishments. The look on a child's face when they are first learning to pee and poop in the potty is priceless. Just like learning to ride a bike, your child may stumble at first. Don't give up! Potty training can be stressful, and you may feel anxious at various times during the journey, but this is normal. Every parent goes through it. Be consistent and stay positive. Soon they will be "riding the bike" with confidence. The first time they are successful using the potty will make all the frustration worth it!

There Is No Right Time to Start

The right time to potty train is when it is right for your family. There is no perfect time. The most important factors are being mentally ready to tackle the journey and noticing readiness signs in your toddler. I always recommend diving into potty training during a "high tide" period. A high tide is when the waters of life are smooth (somewhat), you are getting along (for the most part), and there are no huge life changes (moving, new baby, change in school, new nanny, etc.) that have recently happened or may happen in the near future. "Low tide" periods are when your toddler is showing challenging behavior and life is rocky.

Every Child Is on a Different Timeline

Every family dynamic is different, and so is every toddler. Children hit milestones, like walking and talking, at different ages, and potty training is no exception. It is also normal for children in the same family to be potty trained at different ages, including twins! You just can't rush a toddler or try to get them to do something before they are ready. You may be tempted to worry if other children hit their milestones earlier, but I promise that no one is asking Bill Gates if he was potty trained at 22 or 27 months! Your child's potty-training milestones do not predict their success in life or reflect your worth as a parent.

AVERAGE AGE FOR POTTY TRAINING

While every child is on a different timeline, most children in the United States are potty trained between the ages of 22 and 36 months, with the average age being around 27 months. Also, around 18 to 30 months, you will start seeing your toddler hit many of the potty-training readiness signs discussed later in the chapter. According to Johns Hopkins Medicine, it isn't until around the age of two to two-and-a-half that most children can have control over their bladder and bowels. In helping to potty train thousands of children both in the United States and abroad, I have found there is something magical for a lot of toddlers around 27 to 29 months.

WHAT IF YOUR CHILD IS POTTY TRAINED BEFORE OR AFTER THEIR PEERS?

As parents, it's hard to not compare your child to others. All over the Internet we see filtered images of moms who seem to have it under control, raising "perfect" kids who always look put together and presumably never have tantrums. Don't be fooled by appearances of perfect families on the Internet. No mom has it all together all the time! Likewise, you may have friends who potty trained their child at 16 months and love to talk about it, while others choose to wait until

36 months. It's important to remember, no one knows your toddler and family dynamic better than you do. Trust your instincts. Each toddler is unique, with different needs, habits, and learning capacities. Seeing every child as an individual will help you decide together, as a family, when it is the right time to potty train.

Look Out for Signs Your Child Is Ready

Now that you've looked at age and whether or not your toddler is in a high tide, let's break down potty-training readiness into three categories: physical, emotional, and cognitive readiness. I'll say it again: Every child is different, so please know that your toddler does not need to exhibit every readiness sign to be emotionally, physically, and cognitively ready. Of the thousands of children I have worked with, many did not show all the readiness signs going into potty training and they still rocked it!

COMMON SIGNS: PHYSICAL

I believe one of the most important physical readiness signs in your toddler is being able to stay dry for longer periods of time. When your child can go more than an hour or two staying dry, it means they have stronger bladder control. You'll notice some other physical readiness signs when your child:

+ can walk and run with ease (this does not apply to children with a physical impairment).
+ has regular bowel movements that are well formed (not constipated).
+ pulls pants up and down with little assistance.

COMMON SIGNS: EMOTIONAL

As mentioned earlier, I truly believe the most important emotional readiness sign for potty training is that you are in a high tide with your toddler. You need to be in a good and positive place with your child when entering potty training. You'll notice some other emotional readiness signs when your child:

+ can play independently for longer periods of time (at least a few minutes).

+ dislikes the feeling of being wet/soiled.

+ shows an interest in the potty. This can be through role-playing with a doll/stuffed animal, starting to sit on the potty, watching older siblings or parents on the potty, or talking about using or sitting on the potty.

+ wants independence and control (this pretty much sums up every toddler).

+ takes pride in their accomplishments and/or enjoys praise.

+ seeks to please and enjoys helping.

COMMON SIGNS: COGNITIVE

Cognitive readiness signs for potty training are definitely ones you can work on with your toddler. Playing make-believe games like pretending to be a veterinarian with stuffed animals, playing school, and pretending to have a restaurant are great ways to teach cause and effect, turn-taking, patience, manners, and following directions. All of these skills will be useful in both potty training and your child's daily life. You'll notice some other cognitive readiness signs when your child:

+ has the words for pee/poop (you do not need to use those exact words, but your child should have language for these actions).

+ starts to tell you when they need to go pee or poop.

+ starts to hide to go poop (showing the need for privacy).

+ shows an interest in their body and their body parts.

+ can follow simple one-step and maybe even two-step commands. ("Please give me the book," "Get your coat," "Get me your hairbrush.") You can work on one- and two-step commands through interactive and imaginative play with your toddler.

Some Kids Take Days, Some Weeks, Some Months

Wouldn't it be nice to wave a magic wand over your child and—poof!—they would be potty trained? Unfortunately, there is no magic to speed up the process and, again, every child is different. Potty training will be different for every child as every child moves at their own speed. Some toddlers move quickly and some move slowly, and both are normal. Don't get discouraged if your child takes more time to potty train than a sibling or a friend's child.

Potty training is a marathon, not a sprint! On average, children take between 2 and 10 days to potty train. If you have been working on potty training your child for more than two weeks, you may want to reach out to a potty-training consultant or your pediatrician for tips or guidance, but try not to feel anxious. Being supportive is the best gift you can give your child during potty training.

START TALKING EARLY

Starting to talk to your child about potty training happens long before you actually dive into it. Start by talking about common terms or phrases and using them when your child is with you in the bathroom. Get them comfortable hearing and saying things like:

- "pee"
- "poop"
- "get toilet paper"
- "wipe"
- "wash hands"
- "dry hands"
- "flush toilet"

You can also practice using these terms in real-time conversations:

- "Do you want to flush the toilet or would you like help?"
- "Can you help me get some toilet paper?"
- "Look, Mommy just pulled her pants down and up to use the toilet. Show me how you can pull your pants down and up."
- "Time to wash our hands. Can you give me a pump of soap?"

Talking to your child about what happens in the bathroom will help get them familiar with the concepts involved and also get them excited about participating, which is an important first step to potty training.

It Also Depends on Your Child's Personality

Is your firstborn an introvert or extrovert? Are they strong-willed or easygoing? Do they like to help or like you to do things for them? Do they aim to please? Are they always on the go, jumping from one activity to the next? It may seem that your child exhibits a few different personality types, and that is very normal, especially for toddlers. One minute your toddler may be jumping off the walls and singing their favorite Disney lyrics, and the next minute they're crying when you leave them at preschool. Toddlers are still learning who they are and how they fit in with your family and the world.

Looking at your child's personality and temperament will help guide how you interact with them during potty training. Also, once we look at how our children learn and interact with others, we can start to shape our parenting style to maintain our own sanity and break down the battles we have with our children. Let's take a closer look at some personality types and how they may affect potty training.

PERSONALITY TYPE: INTROVERT

If your child is more of an introvert, they may tend to enjoy playing by themselves or in a small group. Large, noisy groups may be difficult for your child and could induce some anxiety or cause them to stay with you. An introverted child may enjoy reflecting on experiences, and you may describe them as sensitive. Jumping from one task to another may be a lot for them. With an introverted child, we want to tread lightly, acknowledge their feelings, and not overwhelm them. They can be motivated to focus on a task when given praise to guide them. Including individualized charts can help your child feel in control of the process.

PERSONALITY TYPE: EXTROVERT

Extroverted children tend to be busy and on the go. Seeking sensory input and interactions with others are typical personality traits. Your child may seem to have endless energy and love to be on the move with different groups of people and friends. On the other hand, extroverted toddlers tend to "crash" when they are tired—when they're done, they're done. Potty training an extroverted child will include lots of praise and exciting new activities to keep their attention on the task. In addition, keeping your child motivated with "underwear checks"—stopping and saying, "Underwear check!" every 5 to 15 minutes to make sure they're dry—will ensure they are getting the input they need to succeed.

PERSONALITY TYPE: STRONG-WILLED

You may be nervous to start potty training your strong-willed toddler. Thinking about them throwing tantrums and refusing to sit on the potty may make you feel as if you are already on the potty-training roller coaster. Hang in there! Potty training the strong-willed child can be fun. You will want to include your toddler in as many choices as possible while maintaining firm-yet-loving boundaries. Empowering your strong-willed child with choices will help, not only during potty training but also in many aspects of their life. As you probably know, the last thing you want to start with a strong-willed child is a power struggle. Take a deep breath, stay consistent, and give your toddler control over their body.

PERSONALITY TYPE: EASYGOING

The easygoing child—often a firstborn child—may be an avid rule-follower who adjusts to new situations easily. Your toddler may seem so content that they aren't motivated for change—which is exactly why you'll want to offer motivating activities and rewards to make potty training fun and exciting. Potty training can be an empowering time for your child and help them grow emotionally.

Like Everything Else, Potty Training Is an Adventure

Parenthood is an adventure. Parenting a *toddler* is like hopping on a waterslide with your eyes closed, not knowing when a twist, turn, or dip will occur and having no idea when the ride will end. As the mom of a toddler, you know every day is different. Some days you will feel like you have the mom thing down, while other days you may feel like you are struggling. Every mom goes through these adventure highs and lows. Potty training is no different. It's not only an adventure for you, but also for your toddler. This is one of the first journeys of their life where they will experience pride in themselves.

There May Be Starts and Stops Along the Way

Just like any adventure in life, with potty training you may find that you take two steps forward and one step back. It is normal for your child to have an accident after they have successfully peed or pooped in the toilet. In fact, your child may have several accidents. Your child may also not want to sit on the potty and may "hold it" for long periods of time. You may feel like throwing in the towel . . . only to have your child successfully pee in the potty after days of accidents. Hang in there and use those successes for motivation on the journey. Remember, every potty-training process has these highs and lows.

Potty Training Questions and Myths

You have probably heard several things regarding potty training that you are questioning. There are so many myths regarding potty training, the process, preparing for potty training, regressions, and so on. One of the goals of this handbook is to answer your questions so that you feel prepared, confident, and ready to start potty training your child. Let's look at some of the most common potty-training myths.

1. Girls are easier to potty train than boys.

   NO. This is one of the main questions I get from parents of young children. So many moms have heard that boys are more difficult to potty train that they hold off on starting, even though they feel their son is ready to start. Potty-training readiness depends on the individual child, not the gender. In the thousands of children I have helped potty train, I have yet to find that girls in general are easier to potty train than boys! So, all you boy moms, don't be scared. When you and your child are ready, go for it!

2. I should put my child in training pants to potty train.

   NO. Disposable training pants are basically more-expensive diapers. When you decide to officially start potty training, ditch the training pants (unless you use them for nap or overnight sleep). Training pants are essentially diapers and feel like diapers to your child. They prevent your child from feeling the pee, so accidents will continue to happen. Training pants are not big-kid underwear, no matter what the ad campaigns say. Wearing loose-fitting underwear allows your child to know exactly when the accident is happening, which is very important in the learning process of potty training.

3. Having my child sit on the potty for a long time will help potty training.

   NO. There is absolutely no scientific evidence that shows having a child sit on a toilet for extended periods will aid in potty training. Not only does it not teach them anything, but in most cases it backfires, and the child starts to refuse to sit on the potty. Potty training is a learning process where your child starts to understand the feeling of a full bladder, when it is time to release, and releasing on the potty.

4. My child will tell me when they are ready to potty train.

   NO. Your child has never had to pay attention to bladder control. A toddler's job in life is to play and explore. Toddlers are often unconcerned with diapers or underwear. For many children, diapers are easy and comfortable. A lot of children are ready to potty train far before the decision to start potty training is made. Look for readiness signs in your toddler and don't wait for them to come to you.

5. Potty training is about discipline. I can make my child pee on the potty.

   NO. The one thing I will tell you for sure is that you cannot *make* your child pee on the potty. Potty training is about working with your child and giving them control over their body. If you try to get into a power struggle with your child over potty training, you will lose. Fear and anxiety will only lead to problems and more resistance. You want potty training to be a bonding

time with your child, not a time where you tell them what to do. Children need comfort and support during potty training, and you are their main source for that support.

6. Your child should be day and nighttime toilet trained at the same time.

   NO. This is one of the reasons I started researching potty training several years ago. While some young children can hold their bladder for up to 12 hours a night, many children can't. It is very common for children NOT to stay dry overnight until four, five, or even six years of age, according to the American Academy of Pediatrics (AAP) and the Mayo Clinic. If overnight training is a bit of a challenge, reach out to your pediatrician before trying any night-wetting home remedies such as setting alarms or using pads in your child's bed that vibrate or wake your child if wet. I highly recommend concentrating on waking hours first. Overnight training can happen naturally when your child is ready.

How Will You Know When You're Ready?

Knowing when *you* are ready to dive into potty training with your child is just as important as looking at their readiness signs. Potty training will take time, and it's important that you have that time to spend. I recommend giving yourself a solid three days where you can put work and other commitments on the back burner and focus on bonding with your child. Being in the right mindset is also important, even though it's normal to have some anxiety—every mom does!

Are you feeling positive and ready to support your child through this journey? Can you handle some ups and downs? Are you ready to watch your child take pride in their accomplishments? If you have answered YES to these questions, you are ready to dive in.

SHAKE OFF THE FIRST-TIME MOM JITTERS

So, let's shake off those nerves and dive into potty training. Take a deep breath and remind yourself that:

+ you know your child better than anyone.
+ you can do this.
+ this handbook is for you.
+ every parent has the same jitters going into potty training.

This handbook is here to support you, guide you, and answer your questions. Use it!

DO YOUR HOMEWORK

A big part of calming your first-time mom nerves and feeling ready to tackle a new skill is to be prepared and do your homework. Talk to your child's doctor about potty training and ask them for their tips and tricks. They work with first-time moms on a daily basis, and no mom goes into potty training knowing what to do without help from others or reading books.

Reading books and articles on potty training will give you the guidance you need to shake off those jitters. As moms, when we are unprepared for an event, stress can build and we can start to feel out of control. The best way to feel in control going into potty training is to do your homework so you are ready to tackle this step with your child.

Key Advice:
Five Takeaways from this Chapter

The five most important things to remember from this chapter are:

1. **This is an exciting time in your child's life.** Potty training is an adventure for both you and your child. You will not only have fun bonding with your child, but you will also watch as your child becomes more independent through the potty-training process.

2. **You are not alone.** Being a mom is not easy, and being a first-time mom is even harder. Everything is new, and it may seem like things are changing so fast it is hard to keep up. It's not just you. Every mom feels this way sometimes. Hang in there—you've got this.

3. **There is no perfect age or time to start potty training.** When you and your child are in a high tide and you start to notice their signs of readiness, it's time to dive in.

4. **Every child is different.** Trust your gut. You know your child better than anyone, and you will be their source of comfort and consistency through this time.

5. **There will be ups and downs during this adventure.** Every child responds differently to potty training. That doesn't mean you won't be successful! Shake off those first-time mom jitters and enjoy helping your child meet this fun milestone.

Conclusion

Knowing when to potty train your child is a personal decision that only a parent or primary caregiver can make. As there is no perfect time to dive in, looking at readiness signs will help guide you. Once you've decided you're ready, what do you do next? Keep reading! In the next chapter, we'll cover some tricks and techniques to help you get started.

The First-Time Mom's Survival Tool Kit

Remember, potty training is something you will do *with* your child, not *to* your child. In your potty-training tool kit, staying calm and being confident will be your best tools for success. You will also need to rely on others to help and support you during potty training to help ease the pressure you may be feeling. Communicating clearly and effectively with the other caregivers in your child's life will be a big part of ensuring successful and consistent potty training.

Get in the Right Mindset

Truly, half the battle of potty training is getting in the right mindset. On a typical day, moms have 100 things on their to-do list. The idea of putting everything on hold and focusing solely on potty training can be hard to process. Take the time you need to get ready by reading both children's potty-training books and potty-training guides for parents. This will allow you to see potty training from a child's viewpoint as well as an adult's.

Your Child Will Know If You Aren't Confident

Being in a positive mindset going into potty training is important for you, but it is also essential for your child. Toddlers are smart, and we know that they can see right through us when we aren't consistent or confident in what we say or do. Approaching potty training confidently will allow your child to trust you and the process. Kids look to parents and caregivers for the truth, guidance, acceptance, and love. Potty training is one of the first times in a child's life where they have a chance to show true pride in an accomplishment, and they need your confidence to guide them.

THEY NEED YOU TO LEAD THE WAY

Walking into potty training with confidence will help you lead the way for your child. They will be looking to you for help on this journey. As discussed earlier, there will be ups and downs, and during those difficult moments, our kids need us to guide them even more. They need to know that it is okay to have accidents and that it's safe to succeed as well as struggle.

Reading children's potty-training books with your child helps open up the lines of communication regarding potty training and the steps involved. It is also a great way for your child to see other children or characters using the toilet, normalizing potty training for them. Most children's potty-training books go through the different steps of potty training, from needing to go to having accidents to being successful using the potty. Children are visual learners, and reading books about potty training with them in a calm environment is a great way for them to have fun, spend time with you, and learn about the process. Tip: Always let your child turn the pages when reading to them. Not only is it fun for them, but it helps them learn that when you stop reading, it is time for the next page.

Build Your Support Squad

You don't (and shouldn't) have to go through potty training your child alone. It is helpful to have backup during this journey. Before you start, form a "support squad"—a close group of people to help lift your spirits, talk about challenges and victories, or even grab needed items at the store. Remember, you're ideally taking a few days to focus on *just* potty training, so having people around for support and assistance can help take the pressure off and make difficulties seem more manageable.

FRIENDS AND FAMILY

Aside from your partner, it's helpful to have a small group of family or friends around you for practical or moral support. You'll also want people who will celebrate with your child when they have successes. Having a support squad is a great motivation for kids. They love being able to call Grandma, Grandpa, an aunt

or uncle, or other loved ones to share their success. It's a win-win for both you and your child.

That said, try not to overwhelm yourself or your child with too many calls and check-ins. Let your child be in control of sharing successes with others. If you plan to have friends and family over during this process, take it slowly. This is all new to your child, and too many interruptions or too much excitement may be over-whelming. Accidents can happen when your child gets distracted, so try to keep these interruptions to a minimum in the early phases of potty training.

YOUR PARTNER

If you have a partner sharing this journey with you, it is cru-cial that you are both on the same page. Talking through your potty-training plan with your partner will help keep you on track and consistent throughout the process. It's important for the two of you to be a team and react to successes and accidents similarly so as to not confuse your child. I do recommend having a lead potty trainer, but your partner will be there for backup along with your support squad. On days two and three, you can intro-duce your partner into the routine. This way, you can start to take a step back and not feel that you are in this alone.

POTTY-TRAINING PROFESSIONALS

If at any time during potty training you feel as if you have hit a brick wall and your support squad isn't able to help, I would recommend reaching out for a potty-training consultation. It is very common during potty training to need extra support. I speak with moms daily, and usually with just a 15- to 30-minute meeting they feel much more confident and ready to proceed with potty training. If your child is refusing to sit on the potty or release their pee or poop, definitely schedule a consult or speak with your pediatrician. Some potty-training consultants also offer more personalized help (in-person, Zoom, phone, text, or email packages) before, during, and after the potty-training process. Many families decide that they would like a potty-training consultant to walk with them through this journey, and there's no shame in asking for help! Remember, just as this is new to your child, it is also new to you.

Communicate Clearly

One of the most important things to remember going into potty training is to communicate clearly with your child. This is brand new to your child, and the best way to not confuse them and keep them motivated is to be honest and tell them what to expect. Have words for pee and poop and communicate those to your child. When talking with your child, use statements rather than questions because toddlers love to answer a question with "NO." For example, say, "Tell Mommy when you need to go potty," instead of "Do you have to go potty?" Be direct and use simple words. Remind your child often that they know their body so they start thinking about the feeling of holding and releasing their bladder.

Be Consistent

Consistency will be your friend during potty training (and when dealing with a toddler in general). If your toddler resists your guidance at any time during the potty-training journey, stay strong and positive. Try not to create bad habits that you will have to undo later. Having a written plan will also help you stay on track. This should include the steps you will take, the specific words you will use with your child, how you will handle accidents, and how and when you'll reward your child. For example, if you will be using sweet treats, like Skittles, as a reward, map out how many treats your child will receive for sitting on the potty, going pee on the potty, and going poop on the potty. Mom tip: According to the Cleveland Clinic, sugar should be limited to less than 25 grams per day for a toddler, so keep an eye on the grams of sugar in any candy your toddler gets. You can also include other fun and healthy treats that are lower in sugar such as cheese cut into fun shapes, crackers, or fruit.

This book will guide you through creating a plan to successfully potty train your child. When frustrated, it is easy to give up or give in, and having a plan will keep you consistent. Remember to take deep breaths and reach out if you need to.

HOW TO NAVIGATE FAMILY CHANGES DURING POTTY TRAINING

Although it's best to start potty training during "high tide," family changes like a move, a new school, or the birth of a sibling sometimes can't be avoided. If you are expecting, I recommend not potty training within six weeks of your due date or within six to eight weeks after the new baby is born. Your toddler will need your undivided attention during potty training, and some toddlers may regress when they are potty trained right before a new baby arrives. If you will be moving in the near future or your child will be starting a new school, wait to potty train. If you do have an unexpected change, though, don't worry. Yes, you may see a slight regression in potty training, and this is when it will be very important to stay consistent. Go back to the basics from this book for a few days so that your toddler feels supported.

Take a Break Before You Get Upset

Your attitude during potty training will guide you and your child through this journey. It's very normal to feel frustrated. Every mom will go through highs and lows during potty training. When you feel you are getting frustrated, take a break and give yourself the time to calm down. Stepping away for a few minutes is a healthy way to manage your frustration so that you can return to your child ready to proceed in a positive manner. The last thing we want to do is erupt and become visibly upset in front of our children when they are learning a new skill. Hang in there and never be afraid to take a moment to yourself.

IT'S TOTALLY NORMAL TO BE FRUSTRATED

Frustration is a natural part of learning a new skill. Potty training is no different. As moms, we like to have things in place and feel in control, but during potty training we have to let go and allow our child to take the reins. You will have a lot of moments during potty training that are joyous, and you will also have times when you feel frustrated and want to give up. Please know that you are not alone here! Your child will also feel frustrated at times and you do not want to take away their motivation. You will need to be their rock and their guide during potty training.

Empathize with Your Child (Learning Is Hard Work!)

Being able to empathize with your child during potty training will help them feel secure in their emotions and feelings. When you see your child becoming frustrated, get down on their level and let them know that it is okay to feel sad, frustrated, or angry, and that learning a new skill is hard work. Remind them that you are very proud of them and that you believe in them. As you don't want your child to dwell on the feeling of frustration, quickly move on to a fun activity or something new. Your child will need more hugs and comfort during potty training. This is the perfect time to love on your child and be there for them through the ups and downs.

Don't Put Pressure on Yourself (or Your Child)

Try not to put pressure on yourself or your child during this time. You are doing the best you can and that is enough. You are the perfect mom for your child, and together you will get through this milestone. Accidents will happen. You don't want to put pressure on your child to not have accidents or to speed up the potty-training process. Trying to potty train in a certain number of days will only bring on anxiety for both you and your child. Shake off all the anxious feelings and remember that every child is different.

Focus on Progress, Not Perfection

No parent expects their child to just hop on a bike and start riding without any practice. It can take weeks or months for children to be comfortable riding a two-wheeler on their own. As a parent, you take steps to teach your child the skill of riding a bike without training wheels, just as you are taking steps to teach your child how to use the potty. Don't expect perfection, especially at the beginning. Slow and steady progress over a few days or a week is amazing. Your child will "fall" before they feel confident enough to "ride" on their own.

Potty Training Can Be Fun

Also like learning to ride a bike, potty training is a bonding experience and can be a lot of fun. You can incorporate exciting activities to do with your child, and you will have more one-on-one time than you might typically get. Take this time to enjoy your child. Laugh and play with them. Life moves along so quickly, and we rarely get a few days to just be with our children without all the other distractions life throws at us. Sure, you may have to take a phone call or do some laundry, but for the most part, you will be spending time with your child. What could be better than that?

Enjoy the Process as Much as You Can

You may be daydreaming of sitting on the beach with a cocktail in hand and dreading potty training. I get it! Potty training your child isn't very glamorous or relaxing. But you can still enjoy the process (*and* daydream about a beach vacation). Have fun with your child and involve them in the fun of preparing. Take them to the store to pick out fun big-kid underwear. Your child can also help choose some of the rewards you will be using. Dress-up items are always a huge hit for both girls and boys. If your child is into dinosaurs, look up new dinosaur videos or books to read so that your child stays engaged and motivated while sitting on the potty as well as times in between. You may also want to pick out some fun new drinks or snacks to have on hand—for your child *and* yourself. We want you staying motivated and having fun, too!

Key Advice:
Five Takeaways from this Chapter

The five most important things to remember from this chapter are:

1. **Get in the right mindset.** It's easy to put off potty training your child out of fear, anxiety, or not wanting to put life on hold. Every mom goes through this. I want you to feel confident going into potty training. You can do this!

2. **Have a support system in place.** Tell your close friends and family before you start potty training. You will need other moms and friends to talk to and support you. It takes a village! Don't try to do this alone if you can help it.

3. **It's okay to get frustrated.** Any mom who tells you potty training was a breeze and that they never hit any speed bumps is probably not telling the whole truth. Even when things run

smoothly, it is normal to feel deflated. You are teaching your child a new skill and new skills take time to learn. Scheduling in some "you time" to take a walk, do yoga, or sit and read a book can help you stay motivated. Whether it is before your child wakes in the morning, during their nap, or after you have put them to bed, even 10 minutes a day of time for yourself is important.

4. **Don't put too much pressure on yourself or your child.** Again, this is all new for both of you. You can't rush potty training. Take it one day at a time. Together, you *will* conquer it.

5. **Be consistent.** Staying positive and being consistent are the two most important things to remember going into potty training. Have a plan so you know what to expect and how to react.

Conclusion

Now that you have the emotional skills needed to successfully potty train and you have your village ready to support you through this journey, let's start preparing. Part 2 details the three stages of potty training and what you'll need to manage at each step.

Stage-by-Stage Potty Training

In the following chapters we will look at ways to set yourself up for successful potty training. We'll talk about preparing yourself, your child, and your home for potty training. Then we'll go step-by-step through some key dos and don'ts to help your child embrace potty training and stick with it.

Stage 1

Prepare for Potty Training

Preparing your child for potty training should happen naturally. This is a time where there is no pressure as you let your child take the lead, watch, and learn. Have fun and let your child explore while introducing them to the appropriate language and skills needed to successfully use the toilet.

Key Milestone Advice

Starting early and doing your homework will help you stay confident and not sweat the small stuff when it comes to potty training.

START EARLY

Potty training starts well before you actually potty train. You will start allowing your child to explore the potty well before you expect them to sit on it and release. Let your child have fun! They can help you pick out a small potty and a few children's potty-training books. Let them sit on the potty and look through their new books. This will help them be more comfortable when it is time to officially start.

BE PREPARED

As with any new task, you always feel better when you are prepared. When you do the work ahead of time, you take away the stress of feeling helpless. If you're not sure what to do, revisit the "Do Your Homework" section in chapter 1 (page 16).

DON'T SWEAT THE SMALL STUFF

If you have a child who refuses to poop on the potty, stay calm. This is very normal. Poop can take time, and that is okay. Just keep moving forward, one step at a time. Celebrate the little victories and stay positive. Your child will reflect your energy, so be calm and relaxed.

Potty Training Prep

Preparing for potty training can and should start a few months before you actually begin. If you are reading this book and ready to start now, don't worry! You can take a week or two to go through the following steps. You can begin Positive Potty Associations (PPA) around 15 to 18 months. This will be a low-pressure time when you have fun and let your child explore and role-play. If your child is comfortable, the training will be easier. Listed below are the most important components of PPA.

INTRODUCE YOUR CHILD TO THE TOILET AND SMALL POTTY

I recommend purchasing a small potty before you begin potty training. There are a lot of great options out there—find one you like. Some have flushing sounds and lights and play songs; others are more simple. The goal is for your child to love it, so keep them in mind when purchasing one.

Put the small potty in the bathroom where your child bathes. The best and easiest time to get your child to start sitting on the small potty is before bath time, since it's normal for kids to go potty before hopping in the bath. Without pressure, see if you can guide your toddler to the small potty or even the larger toilet. Praise them for sitting. Use language like "Wow, I love how you are sitting on the toilet. You are such a big kid," and "You are sitting on the potty like Mommy and Daddy." Remember, this is all about positive potty associations—no pressure! We want your child to like getting on and off the potty. You may notice your child stopping by to sit on the potty during different times of the day. Awesome! They don't have to take their clothes off, either. The goal is to get them comfortable first.

DITCH THE CHANGING TABLE

A great way to communicate to your child that pee and poop happens in the bathroom is to make that association early. Around one to two months before you potty train, start changing your child's diaper in the bathroom instead of on a changing table, either standing or lying on the floor. You can do this even if you have a very small bathroom; it's okay if your child's entire body does not fit in the room. Just make sure their head is in the room if they are lying down so they can see you are changing their diaper in the bathroom.

If it's workable, let them dump the poop from their diaper into the toilet and flush. You can say bye to the poop as it flushes down. Talk about how pee and poop goes in the toilet and praise them for saying good-bye to their poop and flushing it. For example, "Poop goes in the toilet. I like how you helped put your poop in the toilet and said good-bye as you flushed it."

BRING YOUR CHILD INTO THE BATHROOM WITH YOU

If you are looking at this and thinking, *Yup, my child already follows me into the bathroom,* you are right on track. Allowing your child to follow both you and your partner into the bathroom (sometimes, not every time) is important, since it makes going to the bathroom a normal thing. If we close the door every time we use the bathroom, our children pick up on the idea that the bathroom is private and not to be talked about. We want an open line of communication with our kids, and we want them to see that going to the bathroom and sitting on the toilet is a normal part of our daily routine.

SHOW THEM HOW TO USE THE POTTY

As we learned in part 1, sitting on the potty is all new to your child. A great way to show them how to use the toilet is to have a dual-size step stool so they can get on and off independently.

Also, when using the potty, their feet should be firmly planted on a hard surface (the floor or a step stool) with their knees elevated above their hips. This is especially important when they have a bowel movement since it puts their body in the proper alignment. Can you imagine how strange it would feel to sit on a huge toilet with your feet just dangling? Plus, you sometimes need to push down with your feet while using the toilet. Our kids need the same support.

ROLE-PLAY

Children learn through play, so one of the best and easiest ways to teach your child about using the potty is through role-playing. Grab their favorite stuffed animal or doll and walk through using the potty with them. Allow your child to be the parent and let them help their doll use the potty while you introduce the language to use. Remember to introduce toileting praise at this phase. You can go over specific language:

+ "Pee" and "poop" (You do not have to use these specific words, but it is important that your child has words for pee and poop and that you use them consistently.)

+ "Tell Mommy when you need to go potty."

- "Sitting on the potty is all new to you. Here, let me show you how to get on/off."

- "Wow, I love how you are sitting on the potty. You are such a big kid."

- "Pee and poop belong in the potty."

- "Let's flush and say bye to our pee/poop."

Role-playing helps you explain to your child what happens when we use the toilet. It also lets them feel in control and confident. Walk through what happens from start to finish, using language like this:

- "Your doll may feel pressure in her tummy."

- "That pressure is her body's way of telling her it is time to sit on the potty."

- "When we sit on the potty, we allow our body to relax and let our pee or poop come out."

- "Our pee and poop belongs in the toilet. Then, our tummy feels better."

ROLE-PLAYING WITH A TOY

Role-playing with your child may feel silly, especially when using the toilet or small potty. I promise that if you make role-playing fun for your child, they will quickly follow along. Role-playing takes the pressure off your child and lets them interact in a fun and safe way. It also helps teach imaginative skills, communication, organizational skills, turn-taking, and much more. You can use role-playing in many different areas of your child's life.

As your child may experience many different feelings and emotions during potty training, role-playing with a doll or stuffed animal and talking through the emotions of joy, anger, fear, anxiety, pride, and frustration lets your child explore those emotions in a safe environment. It also helps take away some of the fear. Here are some examples:

- "How do you think your doll feels about sitting on the potty?"
- "Does your stuffie feel sad or angry when she has an accident?"
- "When your bunny goes pee on the potty, he must feel so happy and proud. Show me a happy or proud face."
- "Don't worry, Elmo, accidents happen. Pee and poop go in the potty."

IT'S SUPER IMPORTANT TO USE TERMS CONSISTENTLY

Using consistent terminology with your child before, during, and after potty training is very important. Talk about the terminology you will use with your partner and any other caregivers in your child's life. You don't want one person saying "go potty" and another saying "use the bathroom," for example. Make sure everyone is using the same statements with your child so they don't get confused. Write down the words you will use so that everyone can see them.

Also, you want to have words for a child's anatomy, regardless of their gender. If we want our children to be comfortable with their bodies, we need to show them we are comfortable talking to them about their bodies. Let them ask questions about their body in a safe environment with you or you and your partner.

USING ACCURATE TERMS FOR BODY PARTS

Talking to your child about their anatomy is an important part of potty training. It helps create a trusting relationship with your child. It also helps them understand their body. According to a 2021 article published by the Arnold Palmer Hospital for Children, it's important to talk to your child about their private parts and label them for your child in a safe environment. You may be nervous to have this conversation, as it may feel awkward, strange, or uncomfortable, but using proper terms such as "vagina" and "penis" helps them feel this is a normal bodily process and they don't have to be ashamed. Avoid cute nicknames like "privates," "peepee," or "fanny." Introducing the topic may feel appropriate during bath time, when your child is changing, or when they're sitting on the potty, since these are times you'll be removing their diaper.

Your Child Will Probably Be Nervous

Just as you had some jitters thinking about potty training, your child probably does, too. This is a new job for them, and while they might be excited, they may also feel uncertain. The more you can stay positive for your child, the more their nervousness will subside. We want to normalize potty training so our children don't get too overwhelmed. Remember, potty training is a normal step in a child's development, and we want them to feel excited for this journey. The more positive we are, the more they can relax and enjoy the ride.

Ahh, Poop!

Poop can be difficult for young children. Some children can have a feeling of "loss" when pooping on the toilet. They may literally feel as if a part of their body is coming out. They tend not to have this feeling when wearing a diaper because the diaper is close to their body, and that is comforting. Also, when sitting on the large toilet, many toddlers feel as if it is a long way down when they poop (and they're right). So, what can you do to help?

1. Make sure they are not constipated. Going into potty training, you want your child pooping regularly (every day or two) with soft poops. Healthy poop means soft poop where your child

is not grunting and pushing for a long period of time. To avoid constipation, make sure your child is drinking enough fluids during the day. According to the urology department at Children's Hospital of Orange County, in addition to milk and juice, two-year-olds should drink two eight-ounce cups of water per day to stay fully hydrated and combat constipation. Constipation and having poop that hurts to come out is the number one reason kids refuse to poop on the potty.

2. Allow your child to use the small potty on the floor when they're first starting to poop on the potty.

3. If using the toilet, make sure your child's feet are firmly planted on a step stool.

4. Give your child some privacy. Many toddlers need a little time to themselves when pooping. You can always make an excuse to leave the bathroom (go check the laundry, grab something, etc.).

5. Pay attention to when your child typically poops. For example, is it after lunch or first thing in the morning? This will help you pay close attention during those times. Many children need to poop after exercising or about 15 to 45 minutes after finishing a meal, as eating helps push everything through the body.

6. Sit down and talk to your child about the importance of poop going in the potty. Always get physically down on their level so they don't feel you are talking down to them.

7. Ask your child why they are afraid to go poop on the potty. Sometimes talking about it and getting reassurance from you is all they need.

8. Run water in the bathroom or play calming music as a distraction.

9. Let them know that you are there for them. Some toddlers want you to sit with them, hold their hand, tell them a story, sing to them, etc.

10. Make a simple poop chart for them and let them help you choose a reward. You can also wrap small rewards like you would a present. Kids love opening presents and the thrill of finding out what is inside is a good motivator.

11. You might try giving them a short, warm bath before sitting on the potty. The warm water can take their mind off pooping and help them relax.

It may take more time than you want or anticipated, and some children do poop on the potty like it is no big deal. One thing is certain—you cannot *force* your child to poop on the potty. You do not want to get into a power struggle with your child over poop. This can cause constipation.

If your toddler still refuses to poop on the potty after trying these suggestions for a few weeks, take the pressure off! Continue to talk about the importance of going poop on the potty but don't force the issue. They are so young, and this is all so new to them. Some kids just need a little more support and time to feel comfortable. Start small by making the association that poop happens in the bathroom.

Here are some tips in the extreme case that your child absolutely will NOT poop in the potty and you have tried everything. Give your child some time to settle into potty training and learning to poop on the potty before trying these suggestions—they are the last case scenario.

1. Allow your child to have a diaper/training pants only in the bathroom for poop. When finished, let them dump the poop into the toilet and flush: "Bye, poop." This phase may take a few days or more, don't worry. You are working on the association that poop happens in the bathroom.

2. Let your child have a diaper in the bathroom and have them stand next to the toilet. You are slowly moving them closer to being able to poop in the potty. After they poop in the diaper, let

them dump the poop in the toilet and flush. Tell them what an awesome job they did.

3. Open up a diaper and put it in the bowl of the small potty. Have your child sit and poop into the open diaper. This will give your child the feeling of having support without the poop dropping so far; they won't feel like the poop is falling out of them. Again, let them discard the poop in the toilet and flush it good-bye.

4. Put the diaper on in the bathroom *very* loosely and have your child sit on the potty and poop. Give them some time—they may want privacy! When finished, praise them and let them discard the poop into the toilet and flush.

5. Cut a hole in the bottom of the diaper (play it cool; don't mention this to your child). Put the diaper on *very* loosely and repeat step 4. Make a big deal about how proud you are that they pooped in the potty! *Do this for several days before taking away the diaper.*

6. Once your child has successfully pooped while sitting on the toilet with a hole in the diaper for several days, it is usually an easy transition to having them sit on the small potty or toilet without the diaper.

If you start to feel that your child is getting constipated or extremely anxious, give your pediatrician a call. I would also recommend a consultation with a qualified potty-training consultant.

What to Have on Hand

One last thing to think about before starting to potty train your child is what you should have on hand so you aren't running to the store at eight p.m. when you are exhausted and just want to sit down on the couch and veg. With so many products out there, what are the must-haves for potty training? Here's what I recommend:

+ **Several pairs of underwear** for your child. I recommend purchasing a minimum of two packs. Children's underwear are typically sold in packs of 7 to 10, so a minimum of two packs will give you at least 14 pairs of underwear to start. You will also want to buy underwear in a size larger than your child typically wears. Toddler underwear is generally sized 2–3T or 4–5T. Opt for the 4–5T, unless your child is very small. This will make the underwear easier to pull up and down, and it will feel less like a diaper. Loose-fitting underwear allows your child to feel if they are having an accident more so than tight-fitting underwear.

  → Try to find underwear you know your child would like, not just what you like. Let them help pick out the underwear, either at the store or at home. You want them to be excited about their underwear, and letting them make decisions really helps them feel in control.

+ **Sanitizing wipes.** Potty training can be messy, sometimes *very* messy. Having sanitizing wipes on hand will help clean up those messes so you can move on quickly.

+ **Dual-size step stool.** This item is mentioned earlier (page 35), but I can't emphasize enough how important it is to have your child's feet firmly grounded on a stool. The stool can also boost your child up for washing hands. Make sure the stool has rubber on the base so it doesn't slide when your child stands on it.

+ **Child-size potty.** You and your child will start interacting with the small potty long before you actually potty train. Also, some children are afraid of the large toilet at first, so having a small potty on hand will help. You can also move it around the house if needed.

+ **Portable travel potty.** You will absolutely want to have a travel potty to bring with you for quite a while. My youngest is six, and we just stopped bringing the travel potty on longer drives. You do not want to be stuck at a park or other public area without a travel potty when your child is refusing to use the public toilet, trust me! Also, *always* carry wet wipes with you in the car.

+ **Waterproof pads for both the car and the bed.** You may want to put down a waterproof pad in the car seat for a while after your child is potty trained. We all know what a pain it is to clean car seats. Also, having a waterproof pad over the bed will save you from changing sheets at two a.m.

+ **A present to give your child at the beginning of potty training.** The next chapter has more detail on this (page 49).

+ **A portable urinal for boys.** As your son will start potty training sitting down, a portable urinal that attaches to the wall is not a bad idea for when they are transitioning to standing to pee or if they refuse to sit to pee. You can adjust the height, which will help you avoid getting pee all over your bathroom.

+ **Plenty of drinks.** We want them to be very hydrated. What goes in, comes out! Be creative and offer your child fun drinks during potty training.

+ **Rewards or treats.** This is discussed in detail in the next chapter. The most important things to remember about potty-training rewards are that you want your child to love them and you don't have to spend a fortune on them. Discount stores are the best places to shop for potty-training rewards.

Key Advice:
Five Takeaways from this Chapter

The five most important things to remember from this chapter are:

1. **Preparing starts early.** Get your child ready for potty training long before you actually potty train.

2. **Use Positive Potty Associations.** You can start working on PPA around 15 to 18 months. Your only goal is to introduce your child to the potty, let them explore, and have fun. No pressure!

3. **Poop can be tough for many toddlers.** Take a deep breath and remember this is all new to your child. Reach out to your pediatrician or a potty-training consultant if you are struggling.

4. **Talk about potty training in a positive light.** Our children are always listening, and we want them to be excited about using the potty.

5. **Prepare your home.** Go over the list of recommended items so you feel prepared and ready to start potty training.

Conclusion

Congratulations! Preparing yourself to start potty training is half the battle. I hope that you are feeling confident and ready to start potty training, as the next chapter will guide you through the first steps in the process.

Stage 2

Embrace the Potty

It's time to get down to business. Let's take a look at exactly what to do, step-by-step, to quickly and successfully potty train your child. We moms don't exactly have all the time in the world to hang out and watch our kids sit on the potty. The goal of this chapter is to give you the skills to positively, quickly, and successfully potty train your child as the two of you bond.

Key Milestone Advice

As you start to potty train your child, you will want to keep some important strategies in mind to stay positive, motivated, and on track. You may create your own goals and milestones with your family, but here are three strategies I recommend for embracing the potty.

PLAN AHEAD
The more prepared you are going into potty training, the less stress you will feel in the moment. You might do things like plan breakfast, lunch, and dinner a few days ahead, or shop ahead of time so you don't have to run out at night or early in the morning. You may also want to have a couple numbers of restaurant delivery services handy.

DON'T QUIT
You may hit rough waters during potty training, but knowing this will help you stay on course. As potty training may not happen overnight, you might feel like quitting and trying again later on. If you are seeing even the tiniest bit of success, hang in there. You may not see success (eliminating on the potty) in the first few days. This is normal. It may take your child some time to start understanding the feeling of holding and releasing their pee. Sitting on the potty, role-playing with a doll, talking about going pee on the potty—any of those may be the victory for the day. If your child makes it to the potty even one out of five tries (even on day three), that is success. Don't give up! Stick with it and every day you will start to notice more small or large improvements.

STAY CONSISTENT
As mentioned earlier, being consistent when you are getting your child to the potty during the first few days will help in the learning process. Have consistency as a goal for yourself during

potty training. When you are consistent in your approach, positivity, and words, your child will be comforted; it helps them feel secure.

Pick a Block of Time to Go Diaper-Free

Potty training takes time, and it's important that you are able to dedicate the time to your child. I recommend blocking out three to four days to commit to potty training and going diaper-free with your child. For some parents, it's not an option to take three or four days away from work or other commitments. Don't worry; you can still successfully potty train your child, it will just look a little different. Don't get discouraged if you need backup!

This is where your partner or support squad can help. The first day of potty training is the most important—it's where you will lay the groundwork. Day one is the teaching day. If you're the lead potty trainer for your child, it's important to be present on day one. Day one may also be the most emotional day, as many accidents could occur.

If you plan to bring your partner or another caregiver into the potty-training process, you can do it on day two or three. Go over everything you have been doing with the new "lead" so that they feel comfortable stepping in.

The Night Before You Begin Potty Training

Take some time to set up for the big day. You'll want to be organized so that things run as smoothly as possible the next morning. Take care of the laundry and last-minute work emails or calls. Here are a few other things you can do:

+ Write your child a note to tell them you are proud of them and you are excited to start potty training. You can read it aloud to them at the start of the day. Kids love to feel valued, and a note is an easy but effective way to let them know you are ready for this experience with them.

+ Give your child a potty present or "potty pal." You can even leave it next to the note. A potty pal can be a stuffed animal or doll your child can have with them on the potty. Many children like to have something to hold when they're sitting there. They can also use the doll to role-play throughout potty training.

+ Set out a couple pairs of underwear on the bathroom counter near the note and present. Choices will be very important during potty training, so always give your child a choice of underwear.

+ Get a good night's sleep. Tomorrow is a big day!

Have Your Child Help You Toss Their Diaper

Upon waking on the first morning of potty training, greet your child as you do any other morning. Instead of going right to break-fast, get them out of bed and walk to the bathroom. This is when you give them your note and present. Make this time as positive as possible. Help your child remove their diaper and say good-bye to it, then let them throw it in the trash. Next, congratulate your child on being a big kid and explain they now get to wear under-wear. If your child would like to sit on the potty at this time, great, but don't push it if they resist.

Let your child choose the pair of underwear they would like to wear. If your child refuses to put on the underwear, don't worry. Try not to make a big deal out of it and try again in 5 to 10 minutes. If your child still refuses to wear underwear, let them go naked from the waist down. Continue to offer a choice of underwear and start to role-play with a doll or stuffed animal so they are in control and can have fun dressing their doll.

Pick out a T-shirt for your child. They can wear underwear and a T-shirt for the first couple days of potty training. Don't put them in pants for now—that's a step you will introduce once your child is comfortable using the potty.

Provide Verbal Reassurance

As soon as you have your child in underwear, talk about using the potty. It's a great idea to start this conversation over breakfast. Keep it calm and cool with a positive tone. Remind them that they know their body and that the potty is right there when they need it. If your child seems scared or anxious, make sure you let them know you are in this together and you will be with them every step of the way. Here are the words you will repeat over and over to your child:

+ "Tell Mommy when you need to go potty."
+ "You know your body. The potty is right there when you need it."
+ "Underwear check!"
+ "Your body is telling you it is time to use the potty."
+ "Pee goes in the potty, not your underwear."
+ "Poop goes in the potty, not your underwear."
+ "I'm proud of you for sitting on the potty!"

The more you say these phrases to yourself before going into potty training, the more comfortable you will be saying them and the easier they will roll off your tongue. You can also make a chart for yourself and hang it in a common area so you can quickly see the terms to use when potty training.

WHY YOU DON'T ASK WHY

Remember to put all your words in a statement and not a question. When you're frustrated, it is easy to get angry and ask *why* your child did something. When you ask your child, "Why did you just pee on the floor?" they may suddenly feel defeated or think there is something wrong with them for not making it to the potty in time. Accidents are teaching moments! We want our kids to know that accidents are a normal part of potty training. Just continue to reinforce the reminder that pee or poop goes in the potty. Try hard to remember having an accident isn't their fault. It could take a few days for your child to start understanding what needing to release feels like and being able to release into the toilet. Here are a few ways you can use statements over questions.

INSTEAD OF:	TRY THIS:
"Why did you just pee on the floor?"	"Your underwear isn't dry anymore. Pee goes in the potty."
"Why did you have another accident?"	"Accidents happen. It is okay. Pee goes in the potty."
"Why are you holding your pee/poop?"	"Let's try to sit and relax on the potty. Grab a toy to bring with you."
"Can't you just keep your underwear dry?"	"Your big-boy underwear needs to stay dry. Underwear check!"

Practice Undressing Near the Potty

A great activity with your child is to practice pulling their underwear up and down *near* the potty. Try doing this when your child doesn't need to use the potty so when they do need to go, they will have practiced this skill. They may need some help with it. Many younger children do not yet have the coordination to master this skill independently. Also, make sure their T-shirt isn't too long. You don't want them to accidentally sit on it as they are using the potty. Children can become very upset if they wet their underwear or shirt accidentally. Keeping clothing loose will help your child feel independent and make it easier for them to pull up or down when they're in a hurry.

HANDLING CLOTHING DURING POTTY TRAINING

The most important thing to remember when dressing your child during potty training is comfort. You want your child dressed in a comfortable T-shirt that they like. Try not to put your child in a new T-shirt during potty training, especially if your child has any sensory issues. You want shirts that have been washed before so they are softer. You can allow your child to pick out a couple new shirts to wear during potty training; just make sure you wash them before you start so the shirt feels more "lived in" for your child. Also, let your child pick out the shirt they would like to wear. You can offer them a choice between a couple shirts, but you want them to be able to have the final choice.

Start to Increase Your Child's Liquids

The more liquids you can have your child drink, the better. So make drinking fluids (not just water) fun! Have your child help you make a smoothie or slushy. Kids are more eager to try something if they help make it. Pear juice is great because the high fiber will help prevent constipation. You can also try using fun new cups or silly straws to encourage your child to drink more fluids.

Learn to Read Your Child's Signs

The more fluids your child drinks, the more will need to come out. This is where you should start looking for signs your child needs to use the potty so you can get them there on time and avoid accidents. Here are the most common signs of your child needing to go:

STOPPING WHAT THEY ARE DOING
Your child may be playing nicely with cars or in the play kitchen when they suddenly stop what they are doing. Their body is giving them a sign that it's time to eliminate. They may start to go pee immediately.

HIDING FROM YOU
This is a very common sign, especially for poop. It's also a good sign, as your child is understanding the feeling of needing to release but just doesn't want to go sit on the potty. Any time your child tries to hide or leave you during potty training, it is a pretty good indicator that it is time to sit on the potty.

AVOIDING EYE CONTACT
If you see your child turning their back to you so that they don't make eye contact, get them to the potty. A lot of kids don't want to see disappointment in their parents' eyes, so they turn away to avoid eye contact. When you are making eye contact with your

child, you are connected. If your child is about to have an accident or already is having an accident, they will not want you to notice.

WALKING ON TIPTOE, DANCING, OR HOPPING AROUND
Children are resourceful. Some will try to pull out all the stops to avoid peeing on the potty. Starting to stand on tiptoe or dance gives their body input and helps them keep their mind off needing to go. If you notice these signs, tell them, "Your body is telling you it is time to sit on the potty." Then, quickly get them to the potty and have them sit.

PLAYING WITH, OR LOOKING AT, THEIR GENITALS
Toddlers think that if they just hold the area, they can keep the pee inside. Also, they will often look down and try to hold their genital area if they have already started to pee, trying to keep it in. This is the perfect time to get your child to the potty quickly so that (hopefully!) they can finish going pee in the potty. Even a couple drops of pee in the toilet is a success.

GRUNTING OR FACE TURNING RED
Many children will try to hold in their urine or poop and may make a grunting sound. Their face may turn red as well. As the brain-bladder connection matures, your child will go through different reactions to try and understand the feeling in their tummy of needing to eliminate. The most common response is to squeeze and try to hold their bladder until they feel comfortable and confident going on the potty.

Use Verbal Prompts

Verbal prompting will guide your child through potty training. When you notice any of the above signs that your child needs to use the potty, say, "Your body is telling you that you need to go potty." Then, get them to the potty quickly and have them sit. You may need to carry your child to the potty to get there more quickly or if they are refusing to walk.

Throughout the day, every 10 minutes or so, remind your child, "Tell Mommy when you need to go potty," or, "You know your body. The potty is right there when you need it."

UNDERWEAR CHECKS

As you use verbal prompts, a fun way to encourage your child to stay dry is through underwear checks. Every 5 to 15 minutes throughout the day, stop and say, "Underwear check!" This is a great time for your child to feel their underwear and receive praise for having dry underwear. To make it even more fun, you can also do "touchdown arms" (both arms straight up with palms facing in) when underwear is dry. Underwear checks are an easy way to start making a positive connection to dry underwear, and praise or positive feedback will help reinforce staying dry.

When They Are Ready, Place Your Child on the Toilet

Since you won't be *asking* your child if they need to go potty, you will be paying close attention to signs to get them to the potty as quickly as possible. Still, accidents will happen. Sometimes a child will have several accidents a day the first few days of potty training, while other children seem to have only one or two. The one thing to remember about accidents is that they teach your child how to hold and release their bladder. Accidents are an important part of the learning process. Your child needs to understand the feeling of having an accident in order to make the connection between needing to go and going in the potty.

When your child is on the potty, don't feel as if they need to sit there for hours. One to three minutes is an appropriate time to sit on the potty unless they need more time for poop.

Many children like something to look at or do when sitting on the potty. There are lots of fun ways you can distract or entertain your child. Get creative!

READ A BOOK OR SING A SONG

A great way to distract your child from thinking about peeing on the potty is to read to them, sing to them, or tell them a story while they are sitting there. You can make up a potty song together and sing it every time they are on the potty. Make it funny and short so it's easy to remember. You can also tell them a new story and build on it when they are sitting on the potty. This is a great time to read children's potty-training books so they don't feel alone in this journey.

GIVE THEM A TABLET OR SOMETHING TO WATCH

Kids love to watch a show or play a game on an iPad or other tablet while sitting on the potty. It really helps them take their mind off peeing. Once kids take their mind off trying to eliminate on the potty, it often happens naturally. You can also use the tablet or another electronic device as a reward during potty training—they get the tablet while sitting on the potty.

It will be important to have boundaries around devices while sitting on the potty. Tempting though it may be, you don't want your child to sit on the potty all day just to get screen time. If they're having trouble giving up devices when they leave the potty, have them help you set a kitchen timer or sand timer for one to three minutes when sitting on the potty. If your child is trying to poop, you can set the timer for five minutes.

HAVE FUN WITH OPEN-MOUTH EXERCISES

If your child is having a hard time eliminating on the potty, try having them blow air from their mouth. Doing fun open-mouth exercises will help relax their sphincter muscles and make it easier for them to release pee. You can also give them bubbles to blow (what child doesn't like to blow bubbles in the house?). Or, have a pretend birthday party and let your child blow out the candles. You can also give your child a harmonica or toy flute to play while sitting on the potty. Another option is a cup of water or milk with a drop of food coloring in it. Give them a straw and let them blow into the cup and watch the color change. Get creative and have fun with different mouth-blowing activities.

PAINT NAILS

A great way to have fun and incorporate rewards into potty training is to paint a toe- or fingernail each time your child sits on the potty. Your child will be incentivized to sit on the potty and have fun while doing it.

WORK ON ABCs AND 123s

You can make learning fun while your child is sitting on the potty. Grab a small whiteboard and some dry-erase markers and let your child practice writing their letters and numbers. You can also give them the freedom to draw anything of their choosing.

Potty Training a Child of the Opposite Sex

Many first-time moms may be potty training a child of the opposite sex. You may have some anxiety about this and think it will be difficult. Hang in there, there is good news for you. You will approach potty training the same way! There aren't many differences in potty training when it comes to gender, but here are some things to keep in mind.

START WITH BOYS SITTING TO PEE

Start with having your son sit on the potty, even to pee. There are a couple reasons for this. The first is that when learning to go pee/poop on the potty, your child will often start to pee and quickly realize they also need to poop. It will be much easier for your son if he is already sitting on the potty when this happens. Also, teaching your son to pee standing up can be messy ... very messy. The last thing you want to do is clean up urine all over the floor while your son learns to aim into a small toilet opening. After your son feels comfortable sitting on the potty to pee and is asking to stand, you can get a portable urinal for the wall to teach your son how to pee standing up.

SCOOT THEM BACK ON THE TOILET

For both girls and boys, when sitting on the big toilet, make sure they scoot back and lean forward. If they are sitting right at the front of the big toilet, their pee is likely to miss the inside of the toilet and come straight out at you! Trust me, this can be a shock to both you and your child. They may also feel deflated that they peed on the floor and possibly on their underwear. Help them lean forward a bit so that it is easier for their pee to go down into the toilet and not out toward you. Having their feet on a step stool with their knees elevated above their hips will help with this as well.

Replace Diapers with Underwear

On the first morning of potty training, have your child throw their diaper away. Some toddlers are very excited to ditch the diapers, while others may have a hard time parting with them. Here are some tips on replacing diapers with underwear:

+ Give your child the power to throw away the diaper and take a step toward the future of underwear. Praise your child for throwing away the diaper.

+ If your child does not want to give up diapers, reassure them. Tell them you know learning a new skill can be scary and that you will be with them the whole time.

+ Don't force your child to put on underwear as soon as they take off the diaper. If they are not ready to put on underwear, stay calm and give them time.

+ Remember to always let your child choose their underwear.

How You Talk to Your Child at This Stage Is Key

Moving forward with potty training is a big step in a child's life, and not every toddler will be thrilled. Diapers are easy. Your child doesn't need to think about pee or poop. They don't have to stop playing to use the potty, and you take care of the dirty work for them. The way you speak to your child during potty training will guide them in how they feel about the process.

CLEARLY EXPLAIN WHAT IS HAPPENING AT ALL TIMES

When talking to your child about potty training, be direct and positive. Let your child know what to expect as you explain to them the process of potty training. You are the teacher. Let them know that they now get to use the potty like Mommy and Daddy. Even if your child is scared and unsure about moving forward, you will be there to guide them. Stay strong and stay consistent.

CHOOSE ENCOURAGEMENT

Always use encouraging teaching words when potty training. Stay as positive as possible. Tell your child why you are proud of them so they know what to expect as well as what is expected from them. Instead of "Good job," try "Wow, I like how you sat on the potty" or "Your underwear is dry, great job."

DON'T CRITICIZE

As hard as it will be to not yell at your child or scold them for having accidents, try not to criticize. It can get very frustrating when your child just isn't getting it or they have accident after accident. You may need to walk away for a minute and breathe. Trust me, I have been there! Remember, you are the teacher—but even teachers need a lunch break to decompress.

TIPS FOR STAYING CALM

If you find yourself getting upset, which is normal, step away for a minute or two. Taking deep breaths in through your nose and out through your mouth while closing your eyes will help you refocus, according to Dr. Jerry Weichman. You can also try 3 x 3 x 3 breathing: Take a deep breath in through your nose while counting to three. Hold your breath for three seconds, then exhale through your mouth while counting to three. Repeat this three times. Try to visualize your happy place while holding your breath. Imagining a peaceful escape can help you relax and forget your frustration. You can also do this exercise with your child. Learning to stop and breathe when frustrated is a life skill they can use in many different situations.

Celebrate Every Success

The fun part of potty training is celebrating your child's successes. Success will come in different forms. It could be that your child has dry underwear and you are praising them for staying dry. If your child is having a difficult time putting on underwear and they finally grab a pair, celebrate that. When your child sits on the potty, that is huge, so cheer them on. And, of course, when your child eliminates in the potty, it is celebration time for sure.

When celebrating successes, make sure you tell your child what they did and why you are proud of them. We want celebrations to be teaching moments. Instead of, "Wow, you did it!" try "Wow, I like how you sat on the potty and counted to 10." This will help them keep the behavior going. Have fun celebrating victories in potty training, no matter how small they may seem.

Key Advice:
Five Takeaways from this Chapter

This was a big chapter with a lot of information. The five most important things to remember from this chapter are:

1. **Give your child the power to ditch their diapers.** When you both wake up on the first morning of potty training, let your child throw the diaper in the trash and tell them how proud you are. Then, allow your child to choose the underwear they want to wear. Choices are huge for a toddler. They help your child feel in control. They are a big kid now!

2. **Choose your words wisely.** Use statements, not questions. When potty training, don't ask your child, "Do you have to go potty?" Instead, say, "Tell Mommy when you need to go potty." You will repeat this many, many times while potty training and for some time after as well. You are giving your child the power to start understanding their body.

3. **Learn your child's signs for needing to use the potty.** This is a very important step. Catching your child in the act of having an accident and getting them to the potty helps the learning process. Review the signs from earlier in the chapter and be present with your child when potty training, as accidents happen quickly.

4. **Have fun with your child while they are sitting on the potty.** The more enjoyable it is for your child to use the potty, the more they'll want to do it. You can also use a kitchen timer while your child is sitting on the potty, so your child knows there is a start and an end to the activity.

5. **Use teaching words and have fun celebrating your child's successes.** We want our children to understand the *why* behind each celebration.

Conclusion

Now you know what to say and what to look for when you start your potty-training journey with your child. Be consistent, stay positive, use statements (not questions), and have fun. Celebrate the small and large successes and enjoy finding what works for your child. Next, we will explore how to personalize potty training to meet the individual needs of your child.

Keep Going!

You are doing a great job! Now it is time to keep going. When you feel like your child keeps falling off the bike, pick them back up. They are learning and becoming more confident with every success. Figuring out what works for your child and which reward system you are both comfortable with will make potty training more enjoyable and successful.

In this chapter, we will take a closer look at personalizing potty training for you and your child. We'll also talk about when and why accidents most commonly occur so you'll have lots of solutions in your arsenal.

Key Milestone Advice

Now that you are on your way with potty training, you'll want to make sure you keep making progress. Talk to your child throughout the process and try not to overreact when an accident occurs.

KEEP GOING
You are starting to notice what works with your child and what terminology to use. Keep using the same terminology over the next few days. Keep doing what you found works for your child. Remember—even a small success is a success.

TALK TO YOUR CHILD
Potty training can be overwhelming for children. Don't forget to check in with your child. Ask them about how they are feeling. Let them share with you what is working for them. Always remind them how proud you are of them, even if they are struggling. You are in this together.

DON'T OVERREACT DURING AN ACCIDENT
It is very easy and common to give accidents a lot of attention. Make it a goal to take two breaths before reacting to an accident. Allowing yourself to breathe will help you not overreact or say something to your child that you'll regret later. Also, when you overreact to an accident, your child may withdraw and be afraid to sit on the potty.

WATCH WHAT YOU SAY

Our children are always watching and listening to us. They may seem completely involved with an activity, but as soon as they hear us talking on the phone, they zone in to our conversations. Unfortunately, privacy doesn't always exist for parents. We have to be very mindful of the language we use when talking on the phone or to our partner about potty training.

Even if you're not feeling positive about potty training, when in your child's presence, try to avoid talking about any stress or concerns about putting your life on hold, not seeing friends, or having to stay home to potty train your child. Also be careful when discussing the struggles your child might be having, your concerns about how well your child will do, or having to clean up after accidents.

When talking on the phone, let your toddler "overhear" you. It is a great opportunity to reinforce language you would like your toddler to use and hear. You can also use it to drive home concepts you are teaching during potty training.

Here are some examples of positive statements you can make on phone calls if your toddler is around:

- "I am so proud of them and the progress they are making."
- "They are really putting in a lot of work and their hard work is showing in their success."
- "Accidents happen, but they are doing a great job staying motivated."
- "I am loving the time I am getting to spend with them."

You Did It! Now Let's Do It Again

Yay! Your child has had success. You are doing an awesome job, and this is not an easy job to master. Success will look different for every child. Even if your child made it to the potty one out of

10 tries, that is a victory. Potty training will take time, and, unfortunately, it's not something we can rush. They are steering the boat, and it is really on their time.

Be consistent and keep using the same familiar words with your child to encourage their success. In potty training, repetition is your friend. Keep repeating the steps that worked before until your child feels confident using the potty. This could take two days, five days, or longer. Hang in there! You've got this.

FIGURE OUT WHAT ROUTINE WORKS BEST FOR YOU AND YOUR CHILD

Every child approaches potty training differently. Some children will love their new underwear and take pride in choosing pairs to wear. Others may refuse to wear underwear the first few days of potty training. Don't feel deflated if your child doesn't want to wear underwear; it will come. Remember, this is totally new for them. Some children prefer to go commando while learning to use the potty. If this is the case, try role-playing and allowing your child to put underwear on their potty pal or stuffed animal.

Also, while some children like to sit on the potty every 15 minutes and try to release, other children will wait until the very last minute before sitting. As you become more comfortable and confident, you will start to recognize what routine works for your child in potty training. There is no "right" or "perfect" way. The perfect way for your family is whatever works for your child.

GET COMFORTABLE WITH TRIAL AND ERROR

Understanding what works for your child will take trial and error. It may be a while before your child starts telling you they need to go. It may also take some time before they feel comfortable sitting on the potty. That's normal. If your child needs some extra support during the process, you are there. Some children respond well to timers when they have trouble noticing the need to release. If this is your kid, try setting a timer every 30 to 45 minutes or buying a "potty watch" they can wear. When the timer goes off, it's time to sit on the potty. Make it fun so that your child doesn't refuse to leave their activity. Try a "potty pause" or "potty freeze" (page 72) so your child knows that everything stops until they have sat on the potty. Trial and error will be your friend. Get comfortable with watching your child and their cues.

KEEP TRACK OF YOUR CHILD'S PROGRESS

A great way to see that your child *is* moving forward is to track their progress. While it may seem like your child has had 100 accidents in a day, keeping a simple chart might show that it was actually only four. Depending on how much your child drinks during the day, accidents may be few (one to three) or many (more than five). You might also see that there were successes thrown in among the accidents, and that's important. You can keep two charts during potty training—one for you and one to share with your child. A progress chart for your child will focus on their success, and not the accidents. On your chart, you can tally the accidents and successes to see progress over a few days. Also, creating a colorful yet simple chart for your child to hang in the bathroom is a fun way for them to be proud of their success. Let your child put check marks on the chart for each victory.

Use Rewards and Positive Reinforcement

Using rewards during potty training lets your child enjoy "payment" for their effort or a job well done. Potty training is hard work for your child. A lot is being asked of them, so rewards or payments can be crucial. There aren't many adults who would continue to try their best at a new job with no payment for their effort. Our children are the same way. Incorporating rewards or a reward system into potty training is a great way to keep your child motivated.

DIFFERENT TYPES OF REWARDS

There are many types of rewards you can offer during potty training. The most important thing to remember when thinking about rewards for your child is *your child*. What would your child want? Finding your child's currency and what they will work for is the best way to determine what rewards you will offer. There are two main types of rewards: extrinsic and intrinsic. Using a combination of both types, you can praise your child and mix it up with rewards or treats.

+ **Extrinsic rewards** are concrete rewards, things you can physically see or hold. Examples of extrinsic rewards would be small gifts or treats. Keeping what your child likes in mind, you can even use a mixture of small toys and snacks. Ask your child what they would like to work for. Dress-up items are always great, and you can find a lot of fun things at discount or dollar stores. A fun way to keep things interesting is to wrap each reward. The suspense of not knowing what's inside makes it even more enticing.

+ **Intrinsic rewards** are intangible rewards that give your child personal satisfaction. Intrinsic rewards are praise or affirmation, rather than material things you would give to your child. Examples of intrinsic rewards are high fives, fist bumps, and praising words.

If it seems like you are over-rewarding your child during potty training, don't worry, it won't last forever. This is new for them, and you want to keep them motivated. After about two weeks of your child feeling confident using the potty, you can start to fade the rewards. You will want to wean gradually and not cut them cold turkey, which could lead to a regression. If you were rewarding your child every time they successfully eliminated in the toilet, you can make a simple chart so they are rewarded every *second* time they use the toilet, then move to every third time, etc.

Accidents Happen

Accidents are messy, inconvenient, and just plain frustrating. They are also an important part of the process. There is nothing like watching your child pee on a new rug or the couch to make you want to jump out of your skin with anger and frustration. Always try to cover couches with waterproof pads, towels, or blankets until your child is feeling confident with holding and releasing their bladder. You may also want to remove any rugs until training is over.

Remember that accidents serve an important role—they're teaching moments. Without having an accident, it is very difficult for your child to understand the feeling of holding and releasing their bladder, and when and how to do it. Although accidents can be unbelievably frustrating, know that with every one your child is learning, even if it doesn't appear that way. Accidents help your child learn their body's cues and understand their body and the feelings they are having.

COMMON ACCIDENTS

As you start to potty train, you will notice there are common times when your child tends to have accidents. Many times, accidents happen when your child is busy playing, watching a movie, or any time they don't want to stop what they're doing to use the bathroom. Keep a close eye on your child when they are absorbed in an activity, especially when they are watching something, as they tend to be relaxed and distracted.

Also, be cautious about spending time outdoors during the first few days. When children are out in the fresh air, it's easy for them to lose focus and have an accident. Try not to stay outside longer than 5 to 10 minutes at a time the first few days of potty training.

When potty training twins or multiples, you may notice accidents happening when one child does not want to leave their toy unattended out of fear it may be gone when they get back from using the toilet. Always let your child take a desired toy with them to sit on the potty. With twins or multiples, you can also have them go with one another when needing to use the potty. This will allow them to encourage each other and take away the fear of losing a toy while one of them is sitting on the potty.

SOLUTIONS FOR ACCIDENTS

The best strategy after an accident is to stay calm and not give it too much attention. You don't want to keep talking about it or make your child think that it's a big deal or that you are mad at them. Sometimes kids look for extra attention, and focusing on an accident can actually make them happen more often. When your child has an accident, quickly get them to the potty and have them sit down. Even one drop of pee in the potty is a success and will help reinforce to your child that pee and poop go in the potty. Say things like "Bummer, your underwear isn't dry anymore. Pee/poop goes in the potty." Then help your child pick out a new pair of underwear and move on.

THE POTTY PAUSE

If you keep noticing that your child doesn't want to leave their current activity or toy to use the bathroom, try doing a "potty pause" or let your child bring a special toy or potty pal with them. A potty pause or "potty freeze" means their activity stops exactly where they left it and will be there waiting for them when they get back. You can have fun with this. When you notice your child needing to use the potty, shout, "Potty pause!" and stop everything and freeze. Be dramatic. Let your child know that you will stay "frozen" until they use the potty. As you will have a small potty close to your child when starting to potty train, you can freeze while still keeping an eye on your child. Then, you can resume activity once they are done. This shows them that nothing fun happened while they were gone. Just like adults, kids don't want to miss out, so stop the fun until they return. Allowing your child to bring the toy they are playing with to the potty also helps them feel secure and in control knowing where their toy is. They can put the toy on the counter or on the floor next to them, or they can hold it while sitting on the potty.

Handwashing and Other Important Hygiene Tips

Another important step is learning to wash hands after peeing or pooping. Start incorporating handwashing as a natural final step to using the potty. Your dual-size step stool is perfect for boosting your child up so they can reach the sink. Kids love fun scented soap, and foaming soap is easy for kids to use and wash off. Try getting two different scents and let your child pick the one they like. You'll also need to show your child the steps of proper handwashing. Singing the alphabet while washing their hands helps your child understand how long to rub their hands together before washing off the soap. To clean hands effectively, your child should wash for 15 to 20 seconds.

Key Advice:
Five Takeaways from this Chapter

This was a big chapter with a lot of learning tools. The five most important things to remember from this chapter are:

1. **Be proud of the hard work you have put in!** You are on your way. Stay positive and keep going. Remember to tell your child things like "Tell Mommy when you need to go potty" and "You know your body. The potty is right there when you need it." Always use statements rather than questions and remind your child they are in control.

2. **Find what works for your child.** This is a huge hurdle during potty training. It takes some trial and error to find your groove. Does your child like you to remind them to tell you when they need to go? Or do they want to do it on their own? The beauty of potty training *your* child is that you know your child best and you will find what works for both of you.

3. **Keep track of your child's progress.** Not only will you want to see how they have been progressing, but it's also helpful to let your child know how many times they went pee/poop in the potty. This is a great way to motivate them. Even if they only had one success that day, share it with them. Let them know how proud you are of them for making it to the potty.

4. **Rewards are your friend.** Every child likes to be praised and rewarded for a job well done. Have fun with rewards and make them exciting, and always have your child and their interests in mind when choosing rewards.

5. **Accidents will happen.** When your child is learning to pee and poop on the potty, they will have accidents. The more attention you give to accidents, the more they will occur—and the more your child will retreat and not want to use the potty out of fear. When accidents happen, remind your child that pee/poop goes in the potty.

Conclusion

You're on your way now. So far you've been potty training your child in a calm and comfortable environment, keeping distractions to a minimum. You have learned what rewards work for your child and how your child responds to potty training in your home. As time goes on and you start to feel more confident, life may throw you some curveballs. The next section will walk you through the next steps in potty training such as naps/bedtime, visitors, outings, and multiples.

PART 3

Potty Training Next Steps

This section of the book is designed to prepare you for the unexpected challenges that may arise. It will also walk you through potty training outside your home and moving on successfully after you've finished potty training your child. Stepping out into the real world can be scary. The next few chapters will help you be ready to tackle any situation that may arise. Always expect the unexpected during potty training!

Challenging Situations

As you progress through your potty-training journey, you may notice some challenging situations that come up often or tend to linger. You may also notice that your child is regressing a bit after a few weeks or months. Some situations happen very early on in potty training and others pop up much later. This chapter will walk you through the most common interruptions or challenges you may face while potty training. It will also help you figure out if and when you should reach out for help.

How to Handle Sleeping

Dealing with both naptime and nighttime sleep while potty training can be one of the biggest hurdles for both children and parents. You have just spent the last two or more years creating good sleep routines for your child, and the last thing you want to do at this point is shake it up. If you're like many moms, you probably don't have fond memories of those sleepless nights!

Children's Health of Texas has research regarding the importance of sleep on a developing toddler's brain. According to the AAP, your toddler should be getting around 11 to 14 hours of sleep in a 24-hour period. This includes both naps and overnight sleep. Sleep is crucial for the well-being of your child. It helps attention, behavior, emotional and physical regulation, and mental health. If your child is struggling with sleep or you are noticing signs that your child is overtired (cranky, crying a lot, seems clingy, doesn't want to eat dinner, wakes early or has a difficult time falling asleep), reach out to your pediatrician or a sleep consultant. You want your toddler to enter potty training well rested.

Nocturnal enuresis, or bedwetting, is slightly higher in boys than girls. There is also a genetic link. If you or your partner were a late-night wetter, your child has an almost 50 percent chance of also being a late-night wetter. This percentage jumps to almost 80 percent if both you and your partner struggled with night wetting.

In the beginning, you will only focus on daytime potty training. It's not necessary to push for nap or overnight training yet. There are some children that take to both day and nighttime training right off the bat and are able to hold their bladder for 10 or more hours at night. However, it is very common for children to not be overnight trained until they are at least four, five, or six years old.

How to Handle Naps

For both naptime and overnight sleep, have your child wear a diaper or training pants. As soon as you begin potty training, refer to the diaper or training pants as "sleep pants" so as to not confuse your child. Also, get a new look or brand of diaper for both nap and overnight sleep. You won't be using those old diapers anymore, and a great way for your child to feel proud of themselves is to allow them to give their old diapers to a neighbor, relative, or friend who still wears diapers. If you don't know a younger child who fits the bill, you can call Goodwill or the National Diaper Bank Network, or you can try local day care centers for guidance on donating your unused diapers.

For many children, staying dry at naptime happens before overnight training. Many children are able to hold their bladder during a two-hour nap. That being said, start by putting your child in "sleep pants" for naptime. You want your child to focus on relaxing their body and sleeping rather than holding their bladder.

BLADDER HOLDING

If your child is holding their bladder from the time they wake up in the morning and waiting for you to put on a diaper at naptime, you can try to have your child in underwear for naptime. As naptimes for toddlers are typically only one to two hours, this could encourage your child to use the potty before nap. If you go this route, make sure you put a waterproof pad in the crib or toddler bed for easy cleanup.

ENCOURAGE FLUIDS EARLY ON IN THE DAY

You can also encourage your child to stay dry during their nap by giving them most of their fluids earlier in the morning, so their body has time to eliminate before naptime. Always have your child sit on the potty before naptime. Incorporate this into their daily routine so they know to expect it.

How to Handle Nighttime

When it comes to overnight training, don't push your child to hold their bladder while sleeping. Be positive when talking about sleep pants. Make sure your child knows they are a great sleeper and their body needs sleep to stay strong, healthy, and happy. Overnight training will happen naturally for most children when their body is ready. Rushing overnight training and putting pressure on your child to hold their bladder or telling them to try and wake up when they start going pee could make them anxious about sleeping. They may also worry they will upset you if they have an accident overnight.

Remember, just as daytime accidents are common, nighttime accidents are, too, and can last for longer periods of time. Go into potty training knowing that day- and nighttime training are completely separate and may happen at different times. Here are some of the most common reasons your child may have challenges staying dry at night. If any of these issues don't resolve themselves eventually, or if you feel like your child needs extra help, you may want to reach out to your pediatrician.

NOT DEVELOPMENTALLY READY

Many overnight accidents occur not because your child is being lazy and doesn't want to get up, but because the brain and bladder are not communicating. Young children may not be developmentally able to wake up when they sense their bladder is full. Bedwetting is very normal for young children and is considered normal through age seven. If your child is feeling self-conscious about wearing a diaper during either their nap or overnight, try putting a pair of underwear over their sleep pants.

DEEP SLEEPERS

Deep sleepers tend to have more nighttime accidents, as the pelvic floor muscles relax during sleep and don't wake the body to pee. As your child gets older, the brain-bladder connection becomes stronger, and they can hold their bladder for longer periods. Until then, be patient and stick to sleep pants. Once they wake up dry several weeks in a row, you can make the transition to sleeping in underwear.

CONSTIPATION

The bladder and bowels are close to each other in the body, so a backed-up bowel or rectum can make it harder for a child to control their bladder. In addition, too much stool in a child's rectum can reduce bladder capacity, which also makes it difficult to stay dry overnight. For more information on preventing constipation, see page 85.

LIMITING FLUIDS

Limiting fluids three to four hours before bed may be the easiest way to make sure your child's bladder is fully empty at night. If you serve soup to your child, for example, have it for lunch and not dinner. Ditto for ice pops—make those an afternoon snack instead. You never want to eliminate fluids during the day, since staying hydrated helps kids avoid constipation. If you are concerned with your child wetting the bed overnight or want to start limiting how much pee is in their overnight diaper ("sleep pants"), you can shift the focus on drinking a lot of fluids to earlier in the day. The good news is that many children outgrow bedwetting naturally without any interventions.

THE TWO-SHEET METHOD

To avoid changing sheets in the middle of the night, I recommend doing the two-sheet method when your child starts to wear underwear overnight. Set up your child's bed with a waterproof pad, then a sheet, then another waterproof pad, then a second sheet. This way, if your child has an accident late at night, all you have to do is take off the top sheet, and it's back to bed. No one has time to change sheets at 1:00 a.m.!

POTTY TRAINING A NONVERBAL CHILD

You can still potty train a child who is nonverbal or struggles with verbal communication. If your child is showing many of the readiness signs, you can get going. Potty training a child who is nonverbal may look a little different; you'll be teaching them to use sign language and communicate with pictures instead of words. Make sure you have clear and distinct signs for "pee" and "poop" and practice them with your child before starting to potty train.

Using a picture board will help your child feel empowered. You can search online for printable potty training pictures that will go along with the potty-training process (*pee, poop, toilet, wiping, sitting on toilet, washing hands, all done*, etc.). This way, your child can either give you a picture for *pee* or *poop* when they need to go to the bathroom, or they can point to one on a picture board.

You will still look for signs your child needs to use the bathroom and get them quickly to the toilet. Communicate with them verbally and have them use pictures or signs to communicate back to you if they are not able to respond verbally.

How to Handle Medical Issues

Learning how to handle behavioral and medical issues that may come up during or after potty training will ensure the safety and well-being of your child. Some children start very happy and eager to learn, but you may notice their mindset change throughout the process. You may also find that your child, who used to poop three times a day, is starting to hold their poop for days. Staying calm and not drawing too much attention to the issue will help your child not feel ashamed or self-conscious. Pay close attention to your child to notice if their behavior or mental state is being affected. Here are some things to watch out for.

BEHAVIOR

When potty training becomes difficult, some kids will start to act out. You may notice them having accidents for attention, becoming aggressive, or retreating and being very quiet. If your child is starting to have accidents for attention, don't pay attention to the accident. Instead, give your child more attention for staying dry. This is a great time to make a fun chart for your child, rewarding or praising them for their successes.

STRESS

You may also notice your child showing signs of stress, not eating or drinking, or not being interested in you or the activities you have prepared for them. If this keeps happening, try taking short breaks outside with them. Fresh air can help change the mood and allow your child to forget about potty training for a little while. Also, try inviting a grandparent or close friend over for a short visit to lighten their mood.

If your child continues to resist eating or their behavior is very out of the ordinary for them, it may be time to take a break from potty training and talk to your child's doctor. Remember, taking a break does not mean you are giving up!

HOLDING URINE

It's common for children to hold their pee when first learning to release on the potty. The brain and bladder connection may not be fully developed, which could mean your child isn't able to hold their bladder and is having accident after accident, or that they're holding their bladder for extended periods of time. They may also be holding it and not peeing on the potty because they're afraid, and they're trying to control the fear. If this keeps happening, it can lead to a urinary tract infection (UTI) or bladder infection. If your child is holding their urine for four or more hours at a time for more than two days, if their urine smells very bad, or if they're telling you it hurts to pee, contact your doctor, as these may be signs of a UTI.

CONSTIPATION

Some children may hold their pee; others hold their poop. If this is your child, keep a close eye on them. If, before potty training, your child pooped regularly with no problems and now they are holding their poop for a couple days, their doctor may be able to advise you on medications or alternate remedies.

Another sign of constipation is when your child continues to have small dribble accidents with pee. If there is too much poop backed up, it can press on the bladder, making it difficult for your child to fully pee in the toilet.

The longer your child holds their poop, the harder it will be for them to release it. If you notice your child is holding it in, try to get them up and moving. Physical activity can help move things along in the body, and so can the foods and liquids listed here. There are also fiber supplements and gummies approved for kids, but always check with your child's doctor before giving them any.

Foods to combat constipation (can be combined in a smoothie):

+ Pears/pear juice

+ Prunes

+ Apples/pure apple juice

+ Figs

+ Kiwi

+ Citrus fruits/pure citrus juice (oranges, grapefruits, mandarins)

+ Raspberries

+ Broccoli

+ Carrots

+ Spinach

+ Artichokes

+ Coconut oil

+ Avocado oil

+ Sweet potatoes

+ Beans, peas, and lentils

+ Chia seeds, flaxseed

+ Oat bran

+ Almonds, peanuts, and pecans

+ Water

If your child is still constipated after trying these foods, making sure they are hydrated, and giving them time for physical activity, it's time to talk to your pediatrician.

POTTY TRAINING MULTIPLES

The important thing to remember when potty training multiples is to look at each child as an individual. This means noticing the readiness signs for each of them and deciding if they are ready to potty train together or separately. You might think it will be easier to potty train your multiples together, and it is if they are ready at the same time, but you may be creating more work for yourself if only one child is showing readiness signs.

If you choose to potty train multiples together, make sure you have multiple small potties (one per child). As parents, we know that if you only have one of something, every kid will want it! Purchase the same potty in the same color so you can use the potties universally without fighting.

If your multiples are competitive with one another, use that to your advantage during potty training. Have them encourage one another and create charts for each of them so they can see their individual progress. Try not to get discouraged if one child picks up potty training more quickly than the other; this is very normal. As you are teaching two (or more) different children a skill, they will master it at different times. Rarely have I seen two different children master potty training at the same time. You will see ups and downs with each of them and probably not at the same time. Encourage the children to cheer on one another and remind them that they are a team.

If you choose to potty train multiples at different times, let the child who is not being potty trained be your helper and cheerleader for their sibling. Sometimes when you start to potty train one child, the other quickly follows. They start to see the praise and rewards and don't want to miss out.

How to Handle a Child Who Does Not Want to Be Potty Trained

If you have a child who resists potty training right off the bat or who is doing great and then suddenly starts to resist sitting on the potty or starts holding it as long as they can, stay calm. *Don't force them to sit on the toilet.* There are many reasons kids may be afraid to release in the potty. For some it can be the fear of the unknown, while others may not like the sound of the toilet flushing. Some children are nervous because they don't know what happens when they flush the toilet (where does it all go?), and others may think the seat is cold. Getting to the bottom of *why* your child does not want to sit on the potty or why they are holding their bladder is essential in helping them through their fear, anger, or confusion.

TALK TO YOUR CHILD

Sit down and talk to your child if they are resisting sitting on the potty. Sometimes this helps them express their fears so you can find a solution together. If your child is not very verbal, you can use drawings or play a game where they get to choose between different options ("Do you not like the sound of the flush? Or do you not like to sit on the cold potty?"). Children want to be heard. When we get down on their level and talk to them, they often feel safe and comfortable telling us what's going on.

GIVE YOUR CHILD THE CONTROL

Toddlers love to have control over situations, and potty training is no different. If you run into an obstacle or feel like you have hit a dead end with your toddler and they are really resisting, take a step back and give them the control. Remind them that they know their body and show them where the potty is.

Giving your child more control during potty training empowers them to take charge, especially if there is a reward attached. Many toddlers love to take charge, so let them. Pull back on the reminders and statements about going pee or poop on the potty. For some children, the more you remind them to tell you when they need to go potty, the more aggravated they become.

When you pull back on the prompts, your child may initially have more accidents as they are learning to trust their body. The goal of potty training is for your child to become independent in using the toilet. With that can come some mess as they learn. Having plenty of underwear for your child can help reduce your stress about constantly washing dirty underwear. Also, many children love to help clean. Enlist your child to clean up after accidents (with your assistance) so they can share the responsibility and the burden is not all on you. Praise them for their hard work and tell them how awesome they are.

Give them privacy while they're in the bathroom, and make sure you wait to praise them until they have finished peeing or pooping on the potty. Many children can get stage fright if you start to talk to them while they are still in the process of going pee or poop.

START SMALL

If your child is resisting sitting or releasing on the potty, you can also take a step back and start to praise or reward them simply for sitting on the potty. Try giving them a sticker they can put on their small potty every time they sit. Don't worry if they only sit for a brief time; you just want to focus on positive reinforcement for sitting on the potty.

You can also role-play with a doll or stuffed animal. Let your child be the adult and have their stuffed animal sit on the potty. Let your child help the stuffed animal put a sticker on the potty. This also allows your child to be in control, which can break down their resistance to sitting on the potty.

DEALING WITH REGRESSION

Regression is common after your child has been successfully potty trained. It happens for a reason, and finding the underlying cause will help guide you through it. Children tend to regress to a safe time in their life during times of stress or change. They remember potty training as a safe time—they had your full attention and lots of praise. They can also revert to pre–potty training, when they were able to wear diapers and never had to think about going on the potty. Many children will regress after a new baby, a move, a new school, or another big change in their life.

Sit down and talk to your child about the change in their life and how they feel. A lot of times, children will regress in potty training for the attention. They got a lot of attention when they were potty training, and now they are not receiving as much. Try spending 5 to 10 minutes a day of special time with your child to reconnect and show them you are still there and love them as much as you did before these changes happened.

If you feel like you need to, go back to the basics you have learned in this book. Do the same thing you did on day one and start rewarding your child again for either sitting or going on the potty. Praise them for their successes so they feel empowered to continue . Praising your child for a job well done has many benefits. The more you praise your child for positive and appropriate behavior, the more it encourages them to keep going.

Don't worry that your child will become dependent on the praise or rewards they get during potty training. Everyone enjoys praise, and you can continue to praise your child for becoming more independent. Once they are back on track and using the toilet confidently, you can start praising their acts of independence—telling you when they need to go potty, pulling their pants up and down, learning to wipe, and washing their hands by themselves.

Know When to Ask for Help

As moms, it can be tough to admit when we are struggling, but knowing when to ask for help during potty training is essential to your child's well-being—and your own. If, during potty training, you feel an overwhelming sense of stress or heaviness that doesn't let up after a day or two, take a break and reach out to a friend or doctor. Taking a break does not mean quitting; it means you're giving yourself what you need to keep going. Likewise, if your child is showing signs of extreme stress (not eating, not sleeping, refusing to sit or eliminate on the potty), take a break from potty training and talk to your pediatrician. Sometimes taking a break and revisiting potty training when life has calmed down is exactly what you both need. This should be a bonding time for you and your child, not a source of stress. Taking a break to reconnect and trying again in a couple weeks or months can be very healthy.

Key Advice:
Five Takeaways from this Chapter

This chapter was all about how to expect the unexpected on your potty-training journey. The five most important things to remember from this chapter are:

1. **Focus on daytime potty training.** Many children are not ready to tackle both day- and nighttime potty training at the same time. Focus on waking hours first, since that is when your child has the most control over their body. Take the pressure off both of you and wait until your child is ready for nighttime training. Until then, refer to diapers as their "sleep pants" and switch brands/designs. If your child is showing signs that they can stay dry either during naps or overnight, that is great. It is time to try underwear.

2. **Watch for signs of constipation or a UTI.** If your child is holding it on the toilet and you have tried the tips and tricks in this book, it's time to reach out to their doctor.

3. **Review the foods/liquids that combat constipation (page 86).** Sometimes just adding in a few fiber-rich foods can help keep everything moving through your child's system. Constipation is not fun and can be traumatic for kids. Look for creative ways to use constipation-combatting foods in your child's diet.

4. **Give your child more control.** When your child is really resisting potty training, take a step back and allow them to be in charge a little. Let them role-play and be the parent. Add in praise and rewards. This helps break down the battle for control.

5. **Regression is normal and there is always a reason for it.** Finding the reason behind the regression (new baby, new house, new nanny, new school, etc.) will allow you to connect with your child and move past it. Having one-on-one time daily with your child will help them feel important.

Conclusion

This chapter helped answer the what-ifs of potty training. We talked about when to reach out for help and how to move past setbacks and regressions. There is a lot more to potty training than what you do in the first few days. The next chapter will help you figure out how to use the potty-training skills from your household in the real world.

Potty Training in the Real World

You and your child have worked very hard to successfully potty train in your home. At this point, your child is feeling confident and using the potty when they need to. Now it is time to step out into the real world. Leaving the comfort and security of your home can feel scary and overwhelming. You may be thinking, *Where do I start? Where do I take my child if a bathroom isn't close? What do I do if my child has an accident in public? Is my child going to tell their teacher when they need to go potty? What if my child holds their bladder when we aren't at home?*

You will have many questions about going out into the real world with your child after potty training. This chapter will walk you through all the what-ifs of stepping out of your comfort zone and preparing them to be more confident and independent.

How to Prepare for Potty Training Outside the Home

When you are ready to leave your house for outings, you will want to be organized. It can be a bit overwhelming for both you and your child, and having everything in place will make the transition much easier. One of the most important factors to remember is to start small. Take a walk around the block or go to the park for 20 to 30 minutes. Once your child feels confident with short outings, you can start to stay out longer and go farther. If you start small and increase the time and distance as your child is ready, you will be able to easily transition from potty training at home to potty training everywhere.

Day Care/Preschool

If you've taken your child out of day care or preschool to potty train, transitioning back in can happen seamlessly if you prepare your child for the change. Important tip: Talk to the child's teacher before you bring them back. You want to make sure the teacher understands the terminology you are using at home with your child. Let the teacher know what has worked and what hasn't so they can continue using the same words and strategies.

+ If possible, bring in a small potty or toilet seat insert like the one your child is using at home. The more similar the school bathroom is to the one your child is already comfortable with, the easier the transition will be.

+ Create a potty chart to use at school. Your child can be rewarded for using the potty at school just as they do at home. This will encourage them to stay on track.

+ When they go back to school, build in some extra time the first few days to walk in with your child and take them to the potty with you. You have been the lead in potty training, and you are their comfort. Walking in with your child and helping them on and off the potty will empower them to be confident when you are gone.

+ As accidents tend to happen during circle time, free play, or outdoor play, ask the teacher to schedule potty times before these activities.

+ Many accidents happen during free play and outdoor play. Children are often reluctant to leave their games, and they worry that someone will take the toy they are playing with if they leave it. One option is to have the child put the toy they are playing with in a cubby or safe place until they return from the bathroom. If your school or day care allows, let the child bring a special toy or potty pal from home to take to the bathroom with them. They can put it on the bathroom counter until they are finished using the potty. This eliminates the fear of someone taking their toy while they are in the bathroom.

+ Accidents happen! Pack extra clothing the first few weeks of school (or longer). Try not to revert back to disposable training pants at day care or preschool if your child has a few accidents. Some preschools don't even allow training pants, so stay the course! This is a learning time for your child, and it may take them a few weeks to be fully confident at school.

Playdates

Playdates can be super fun, and they're definitely necessary for socializing your child after potty training. They can also be a time where your child may regress and may either hold their bladder or have accidents when distracted. Here are a few things to remember about playdates.

+ Keep it short and small, just like leaving your house in general. Limit initial visits to 30 to 60 minutes.

+ Start by having a friend or two visit your house where your child is comfortable. Once they've had friends over successfully, you can start to take them to other homes.

+ Set a timer so your child has set times to go potty. All children get distracted while playing, and this will reduce the number of accidents. Keep encouraging your child to "Tell Mommy when you need to go potty."

+ When your child does go to the bathroom or sit on the potty, let them choose a toy that goes with them. This way they won't mind so much if they have to leave the fun or the toy they are playing with.

+ Do a potty pause (page 72) when your child goes to the bathroom. Everything—all the fun and all the playtime—stops until after your child has used the potty. Have fun and be dramatic.

Other Caregivers

When leaving your child with another caregiver, your main goal will be to update that person on exactly what you have been doing with potty training. The last thing you want after all that time is to leave your child with someone who isn't reinforcing your methods. In that situation, your child can regress or develop bad habits. Writing everything down is a great way to ensure the caregiver understands your child's potty-training goals and procedures.

FAMILY AND FRIENDS

Family and friends will be excited to share your child's joy at becoming a big kid. Just like going on outings, start small with family and friends. Do not overwhelm your child with a huge family party soon after potty training. Start by having one or two family members over, and gradually, over several weeks, you can bring more people in.

When you have company, pay extra attention to your child. If your child has been potty trained for less than a few months, it is still new to them. They're still learning their body's cues that tell them when they need to go. Accidents will happen, especially when kids are distracted. So, just take it slow and have fun!

Public Restrooms

Most adults do not love using public restrooms. Expecting our children to like them or use them easily is a lot to ask. Here are some tips and tricks to use when introducing your child to public restrooms.

+ Start with a familiar restroom where you've gone with your child before. This may be at a public park, grocery store, or mall where they have seen you use the restroom. This will be familiar to them, and familiar equals comfort.

+ Carry a travel potty with you if your child absolutely refuses to use public restrooms. You don't want them holding their bladder. If you have an emergency travel potty, your child will continue on their successful potty-training journey.

EMERGENCY SUPPLIES TO KEEP ON HAND

Congratulations! You're starting to venture out of your house. Make sure you keep some emergency supplies with you or in your car. It is always better to be overprepared than underprepared.

- **A few pairs of underwear and a change of clothes,** even if you're only going to the store and back. Carry the spare clothes in a resealable plastic bag that can double as a place to put soiled clothing, keeping it away from everything else.
- **Disposable wipes.** Always have wipes on hand for restrooms that are out of toilet paper or if your child doesn't like the feel of the toilet paper. Many children with sensory processing issues may not want to touch the toilet paper in public restrooms. Flushable wipes will also come in handy if your child needs to poop.
- **Hand sanitizer.** Many public restrooms or portable potties do not have soap dispensers, or they tend to be empty. As you know, newly potty-trained children aren't the best at wiping and tend to touch everything. Hello, mess! You want them to have clean hands leaving a public restroom.

If you can't immediately get to a bathroom when your child needs to go, stay calm and be creative. Tell your child that you will get to a bathroom as soon as possible and think of a distraction to take their mind off of needing to go. Sing their favorite song, count with them, or tell a story.

In the Car

Traveling in the car with a newly potty-trained toddler brings its own set of challenges, but there are simple steps you can take to feel prepared. Here are some tips to get through your car ride mess-free.

+ Carry a travel potty in your car for emergencies. If you can't get to a public restroom or your child won't use one, you do not want them holding their bladder or having an accident. Also, during longer road trips, you can pull off the road and quickly pop up the potty in the trunk of your car.

+ Keep a waterproof pad on the car seat. A wet or soiled car seat can be tough to clean, and you don't want your child sitting in a wet car seat if they have had an accident and there's a long ride ahead.

On an Airplane or Train

Travel can actually be enjoyable if you are prepared and understand what you are getting into. Traveling on an airplane or train is like combining long car rides with lots of people and public restrooms. So, being prepared will not only keep your child on track with their potty training but will also help reduce any anxiety or fear they (or you!) may feel.

Always have your child use the bathroom at the airport or train depot right before boarding. After boarding and before taking off, walk your child to the bathroom so they can see where they will be peeing or pooping if needed.

Have diapers on hand and put a diaper ("sleep pants") on your child before they take a nap. If you will be traveling at night, put your child in a diaper before boarding—it's one less thing to think about while you're on the plane/train.

MANAGING THOSE SCARY AUTOMATIC FLUSH TOILETS

Automatic flush toilets can be very scary and loud for children. Many children may cover their ears in a public bathroom, even if the flush is from the stall next to them. Often, children are so small that they trigger the automatic flush while they are still sitting on the potty. If your child is sitting on a toilet trying to pee or poop when the automatic flush starts, it can be traumatic for them. They may not be too willing to sit on another public toilet for a while after that.

One way to handle this is to carry sticky notes in your purse. Cover the automatic flush sensor before your child sits on the toilet. Then, once your child is finished and off the toilet, you can remove the sticky note and the toilet will flush.

Key Advice:
Five Takeaways from this Chapter

Venturing from your house with your child after potty training can be tricky. The five most important things to remember from this chapter are:

1. **Get your child's teacher on the same page.** When your child returns to school or day care after potty training, talk to their teacher so they can model what you're doing at home. This will help your child be successful in the new environment. If possible, walk your child into school for a few days and help them use the potty until they feel comfortable doing it on their own.

2. **With playdates or family visits, start small and short.** Your child will be excited to share their potty-training success with friends and other family members. Start with one or two people for a short amount of time (30 to 60 minutes). As your child feels more comfortable, you can increase both the number of people and the time you spend together.

3. **Public restrooms may feel scary or different for your child.** To help them go potty in a new environment, start with a bathroom they have seen before and are comfortable with. Always have a travel potty in your car in case your child refuses to sit on an unfamiliar potty.

4. **Keep a waterproof pad on the car seat.** Having a waterproof pad in your child's car seat can save you from totally dismantling their car seat to wash if they have an accident. Always have your child sit on the potty before leaving the house and start with short car trips.

5. **Travel prepared.** When leaving the house, make sure you have a travel potty, wipes, and a change of clothing with two to three pairs of extra underwear. Keep the clothing in a resealable plastic bag and use it afterward to keep soiled clothing separated.

Conclusion

Stepping out into the real world after being able to control the environment at home can take some time and planning. It's worth the effort to help your child continue to be successful (and stay dry!) on their potty-training journey. The good news is that, with the steps from this chapter, you will be prepared to tackle the unexpected. If you still have questions, keep reading. The next section will answer the most commonly asked questions about potty training.

PART 4

Real–Life Situations and FAQs

During and after potty training, a lot of questions may arise. In this section, you'll find some of the most frequently asked potty-training questions from first-time moms. These questions and answers address a variety of real-life scenarios that you may encounter.

Q **My toddler starts crying every time we have to use a public restroom. He has a real fear of using a bathroom that is new to him. What can I do?**

A Leaving the comfort of your own home and using a public restroom can be very scary and intimidating for children. The sounds, the lights, and the different toilets may be difficult for your child soon after being potty trained.

When introducing your child to a public restroom, start with one that is familiar to them—a restroom where they have been before and that they have seen you use in the past. Before they sit on the toilet, you should sit first so they can watch you. When children see a parent do something first, it helps normalize the situation and takes the fear away. Know that it may take a few trips before your child is willing to sit on a new potty. Carry a travel potty in case your child isn't ready to use the public toilet.

Before you go in, talk to your child about using the public restroom. Ask them what is making them nervous or afraid. Let them know that you are right there with them and you won't leave them. You can also remind them that you will cover the automatic flush sensor so it won't flush while they're sitting on the toilet (the loud noise tends to scare kids). The first few times, have a small surprise ready for them after they use the toilet. Let them know you are so proud of them and that you have a surprise waiting.

Q We have to keep my toddler in diapers when she visits her grandmother because she has an accident every time. This is really getting in the way of a consistent potty-training routine. Help!

A New environments and different people can cause regressions and anxiety in newly potty-trained children. The routine at Grandma's house is new and fun, with different toys and activities, and toddlers can be easily distracted. This makes it easier for them to forget about bladder control and have an accident.

Have your child wear underwear. You don't want to confuse your child by putting diapers on them at Grandma's house. Take the time to talk to Grandma about your child's potty-training routine and the signs that they need to go. Let her know what's been working for your child so she can replicate it. Bring the small potty from your house so that your child has a familiar toilet. Before leaving your child at Grandma's, take them with you to the bathroom and have them try to go potty. Remind your child that it's important to keep their underwear dry. You may also want Grandma to set a timer for 45 minutes the first few times your child goes to her house. This will remind both Grandma and your child that it is time to use the bathroom.

Q   **I started potty training, and my child just keeps peeing on themselves and doesn't seem to care. Help!**

A   For most children, potty training does not happen overnight. It is so common for children to have several accidents at the start of potty training. Accidents are an important part of potty training—they help children learn how it feels to release urine without a diaper on. Going from wearing diapers (where they never have to think about bladder control) to underwear (where they need to think about it constantly) will take some time to fully develop.

It may take some children a few weeks just to *start* understanding the feeling of holding and releasing. A lot of learning needs to take place, and the feeling comes with time and practice.

Remember to put your child in underwear a size larger than they typically wear. Looser underwear allows your child to feel the accident quickly and is easier to pull up and down. If accidents continue, try removing the underwear for a few days. With the underwear gone, the body has the full sensation of peeing and having an accident. Also, some children will continue to poop in underwear because they know the underwear will catch the poop. Your child is less likely to have a poop accident if they are naked.

Let your child help pick out their new underwear and talk about the importance of keeping it dry. Underwear checks will also help motivate your child to stay dry. Praise them for having dry underwear. This gives them a positive association with staying dry. The more you can stay positive, reinforce that pee goes in the potty, and help your child take pride in keeping their underwear dry, the less likely it is that accidents will occur.

Q How should my son transition from sitting to pee to standing?

A Many times the transition from sitting to pee to standing will happen naturally as your son gets more comfortable using the toilet and understanding the feeling of needing to pee versus poop. When a child is learning to use the toilet, they may think at first that they only need to pee, but when they sit, they find they need to poop as well. With time, your child will get better at navigating these feelings. Many boys find it easier to sit to pee and don't transition to standing for a few months or more.

When your son starts asking about standing to pee, it is time to transition him to standing. I'd suggest starting with a portable urinal you can attach to the bathroom wall. You can adjust the height to fit your son. Once he is successful using the urinal, he can start peeing in the toilet standing up. You may need to use a step stool, depending on your son's height, so his feet are planted firmly on the ground and he isn't standing on tiptoe. Let your son know that he will always sit to poop and stand when he needs to pee. Remind him that if he isn't sure if he needs to poop, then he should sit so he doesn't have an accident standing.

You will need to show him how to point his penis down when he pees. If you do not want urine all over the bathroom, make sure to help your son position his body straight on the toilet. Try not to talk to him while he is peeing so that his body stays in position. With practice, your son will learn to stand to pee and sit to poop.

Q When should my child start wiping themselves?

A You can start to work on wiping as soon as you start potty training. Many children are too small to reach their arms around their body to properly wipe. It may take your child some time, even a couple years, to be able to wipe well, depending on their size.

You can start by having them get the toilet paper and fold it in half twice. You do not want them crumpling up the toilet paper; you want them to learn to fold it twice for extra protection. You'll need to show them how to grab an appropriate amount of toilet paper so as not to clog the toilet. Many kids *love* to grab a lot of toilet paper, so keep an eye on this.

Always teach your daughter to wipe front to back. You can demonstrate and have your child help by putting their hand over yours as you teach them to wipe. As poop can be messy, using a disposable wet wipe will be the easiest way to teach your child to wipe poop. Flush only one wipe at a time as to not clog the toilet. Be patient and know that wiping properly is a learned skill.

Q How do I potty train a child who goes to day care full-time?

A As the majority of the training will be done the first few days, you can still potty train a child who attends preschool or day care full-time. You will want to wait for a long weekend or break to start potty training to give yourself an extra day. Staying in close communication with your child's teacher so you can talk about successes and struggles and what has been working at home with your child will be the key to your child's success.

After you have finished three to four days of potty training at home, send your child back to day care in underwear (if possible). Sending your child back to day care in disposable training pants could confuse your child and cause a setback. Accidents may happen at day care. That's okay. Keep communicating with your day-care provider so that your child feels as comfortable as possible going back to day care and using the toilet successfully.

Q My three-year-old is going potty just to watch videos on my iPhone. How do I break this habit?

A Many children will enjoy being able to have screen time while seated on the potty. That said, you will need to have some boundaries. If your child only wants to sit on the potty so that they can use your phone, start setting time limits for sitting on the potty.

Get a kitchen timer or sand timer and set it for one to three minutes. That is a reasonable time for your child to sit on the potty. They may need a bit more time (up to five minutes) if they are trying to poop. Have your child set the timer so they are in control. When the timer goes off or the sand is gone, it's time to give back the electronics and leave the bathroom.

If your child continues to say they need to use the bathroom to get some screen time, set a timer in the common area for 30 to 45 minutes. When the timer goes off, it is time for your child to sit on the potty. You can do this for up to two weeks while your child is getting comfortable with potty training. Then, start to wean from the timer or set the timer for longer periods until your child starts to take control and tells you when they need to go.

Q My daughter waits until she goes pee a little bit in her underwear to tell me she needs to use the potty.

A Potty training is a marathon, not a sprint. When children are learning the sensation of needing to pee or poop and holding their bladder, it is not uncommon for them to go a little bit in their underwear and then realize what is happening, stop, and tell you they need to go potty. This can continue for a week or two, and it is very common for some accidents to occur up to six months to a year after potty training.

 If your child continues to have small accidents in their underwear before telling you they need to go pee, remove the underwear for a few days. They may need to be naked from the waist down to fully understand the feeling of releasing pee. When your child starts to stay dry until potty time, you can reintroduce underwear.

Q Should I put my child in training underwear when we are out of the house?

A No! Training underwear (padded underwear) should not be used at any time during or after potty training. Potty training underwear or underwear with extra padding feels like a diaper to your child. Yes, it can be scary venturing out with your child after potty training, but you don't want to send them mixed messages. If you're worried about your child having an accident in public, pack extra clothes instead.

 Start with small and short outings so your child can gain the confidence they need to continue being successful when out of the house.

Q Is there value in hiring a potty-training consultant?

A The short answer is yes! Potty training is a milestone that every child must tackle, and unless you read books on the topic and reach out for help, it can be very confusing and frustrating. There are many options to choose from when hiring a potty-training consultant, including phone consultations, text or email check-ins, and all-inclusive packages that hold your hand and walk your family through the potty-training journey. Potty training consultants can help take the pressure off and be there to answer any questions that may arise.

Q I am due in a few months with our second child, and my toddler is showing signs of readiness. Should I potty train before or after the baby arrives?

A Timing when to potty train your child if you are expecting a new baby will take some planning. I recommend potty training either two to three months before the baby arrives or waiting two to three months after the baby is born.

If you choose to move forward with potty training before the new baby arrives, you'll need that amount of time to get your child feeling confident before the baby arrives. Potty training right before the new baby arrives may result in your toddler trying to revert to being a baby after the baby is born.

Before welcoming a new baby, you may be very tired and feel a bit overwhelmed. If thinking about potty training your child before the new baby arrives is a lot for you to handle, wait until after the baby is born.

If you plan to be home with the new baby two to three months after birth, this could also be a nice, quiet time to potty train your toddler. Do what works for your family. Don't feel pressured to potty train your toddler before the new baby arrives. But, if you feel ready to potty train a few months before the new baby is due, go for it!

A Final Note

Congratulations! You have made it through the book, and you now have the tools needed to successfully potty train your child. You know your child better than anyone, so the right time to potty train will be when you feel you are both ready. I want you to feel empowered heading into potty training as this is a large milestone in your child's life and a wonderful bonding time for you and your child. Go into potty training during a high tide when life is calm. You've got this!

Always reach out to friends or professionals when questions arise. Have fun, be positive, and stay consistent. Let's POTTY, mamas!

Resources

Instagram

@healthiest_baby
Expert parenting advice for your baby's first years from a pediatrician and trained midwife.

@lifeofdrmom
A health and medical blog for new moms written by a doctor of family medicine.

@playtalklove
A pediatric speech-language pathologist (SLP) provides practical tips for supporting the language growth of your baby and toddler.

@speechmamas
Two speech therapists and moms offer tips on teaching your child to talk.

@teachtalkinspire
A former teacher shares educational activities for before and after naptime.

@toddlerworks
A parent mentor and educator helps you develop socio-emotional skills and play-based learning with your toddler.

@transformingtoddlerhood
This page provides positive, respectful, and developmentally appropriate tools for your toddler.

Websites

BabyCenter.com
A parenting resource for families with children up to age eight.

Fatherly.com
A digital lifestyle brand geared toward dads but helpful for all parents and caregivers, providing news, expert advice, product recommendations, and other resources.

HealthyChildren.org
The American Academy of Pediatrics (AAP) parenting website backed by 67,000 pediatricians committed to the attainment of optimal physical, mental, and social health and well-being for all infants, children, adolescents, and young adults.

NationalDiaperBankNetwork.org
The National Diaper Bank Network (NDBN) provides basic necessities required to build the strong foundations all children, families, and individuals need to thrive and reach their full potential.

Parenting.com
A website that covers everything parenting-related, from pre-baby through childhood.

PositiveDiscipline.com/free-downloads
This site offers helpful resources to parents during times when they're working remotely.

RaisingChildren.net.au/pregnancy/health-wellbeing /healthy-lifestyle/pelvic-floor-care
This site provides diagrams and information on the pelvic floor and how it works.

**TheEverymom.com/what-you-need-to-know-about
-pelvic-floor-function-in-kids**
This resource tells you what you need to know about the importance of pelvic floor function in children during potty training.

Potty Training Books for Kids

Princess Potty by Samantha Berger

Everyone Poops by Taro Gomi

A Potty For Me! by Karen Katz

Potty Time with Elmo by Kelli Kaufmann

References

American Academy of Pediatrics. "Bedwetting in Children and Teens: Nocturnal Enuresis." Last modified June 26, 2019. healthychildren.org/English/health-issues/conditions /genitourinary-tract/Pages/Nocturnal-Enuresis-in -Teens.aspx.

American Academy of Pediatrics. "Toilet Training." Accessed March 11, 2021. aap.org/en-us/advocacy-and-policy /aap-health-initiatives/practicing-safety/Pages/Toilet -Training.aspx.

Children's Health. "Your Child's Sleep Affects Their Brain." Accessed March 26, 2021. childrens.com/health-wellness /your-childs-sleep-affects-their-brain.

CHOC Children's. "How Much Water Should Kids Drink?" Accessed March 25, 2021. choc.org/programs-services /urology/how-much-water-should-my-child-drink.

Cleveland Clinic. "What to Do When Your Child Eats Too Much Sugar." March 26, 2020. health.clevelandclinic.org/what-to -do-when-your-child-eats-too-much-sugar.

Johns Hopkins Medicine. "Toilet Training." Accessed March 25, 2021. hopkinsmedicine.org/health/wellness-and-prevention /toilettraining.

Mayo Clinic Staff. "Potty Training: How to Get the Job Done." Mayo Clinic. October 5, 2019. mayoclinic.org/healthy-lifestyle /infant-and-toddler-health/in-depth/potty-training/art -20045230.

Schmidt, Courtney. "How and Why to Talk to Your Kids about Their Private Parts." Arnold Palmer Hospital for Children. March 29, 2018. arnoldpalmerhospital.com/content-hub /how-and-why-to-talk-to-your-kids-about-their -private-parts.

Sisson, Kathy. "What You Need to Know About Postpartum Pelvic Floor Wellness." The Everymom. July 23, 2019. theeverymom .com/what-you-need-to-know-about-postpartum -pelvic-floor-wellness.

UNC School of Medicine Department of Urology. "Daytime Wetness, Nighttime Bedwetting, and Constipation." Accessed March 11, 2021. med.unc.edu/urology/pediatrics/pediatric -conditions/daytime-wetness.

Urology Care Foundation. "Nocturnal Enuresis (Bedwetting)." Accessed March 11, 2021. urologyhealth.org/urologic -conditions/bed-wetting-(enuresis).

Weichman, Jerry. *How to Deal: Real-World Tools for Surviving Your Teenage Years.* 2nd ed. Lulu.com, 2013.

Index

P

Pee, 8, 59
  automatic flush toilets, use of, 102
  boys, peeing standing up, 58, 109
  handwashing after peeing, 72–73
  open-mouth exercises as helping to
    release urine, 57
  prompts and reminders, 22, 36, 50, 51,
    55, 62, 73, 98
  questions and myths regarding, 12–13
  signs of needing to pee, 7, 53–54
  travel, peeing during, 101
  UTIs and over-holding urine, 85
  See also Accidents; Bladder control
Playdates, 97–98, 103
Poop, 8, 56, 59
  automatic flush toilets, use of, 102
  boys, sitting to poop, 58, 109
  nonverbal children, indicating need
    to poop, 83
  poop accidents, 11, 71, 74, 108
  regular bowel movements, 5
  reluctant poopers, 22, 33, 41–42
  sensations of needing to
    poop, 53–54, 112
  sitting on toilet, time spent
    in, 56, 57, 111
  step stools, using during bowel
    movements, 36
  travel, pooping during, 101
  wet wipes, use of, 100, 110
  See also Handwashing
"Poop goes in the potty" concept,
  35, 37, 38, 40, 50, 51, 71, 74
Positive Potty Associations
  (PPA), 34, 45
Potty books, 20, 33, 56
Potty charts, 50, 70
  motivational factor, 9, 41, 73
  for preschool use, 96
  progress charts, 68, 84
  for twins/multiples, 87

Potty freeze/pause, 68, 72, 98
Potty toys, 36, 37–38, 49, 67, 72, 97, 98
Potty training, 7, 16, 26, 90
  average age for training, 4
  child's signs, learning to
    read, 53–54, 62
  clothes, handling during potty
    training, 52
  first morning of, 49, 61
  initial outings, 96, 99, 103
  key milestone advice, 33, 47–48
  mindset, building up for, 19, 27, 65
  must-haves for success, 43–44
  personality types, adjusting for, 9–11
  resistance to, how to handle, 88–89
  three-four days, dedicating training
    to, 15, 48
  time limits for sitting on potty, 57, 111
  toilet, scooting back on, 58–59
  toilet training myths, 12–14
  two to ten days to potty train as
    typical, 8
Potty training consultants, 8, 22,
  42, 45, 113
Potty-training books for kids, 20, 118
Preschool, 96–97, 110
Privacy, providing, 7, 40, 42, 89
Public restrooms, 99, 103, 106

R

Readiness signs
  average age for potty training, 4
  cognitive readiness signs, 7
  common signals, 5–6
  in "high tide" periods, 3, 6, 17
  in multiples, 87
  myths regarding, 12, 13
  new baby, delaying training
    due to, 113
  of nonverbal children, 83
  parents, feeling ready to train, 15
Regression, 12, 90, 97

Acknowledgments

Helping moms is my passion, and I love working with families to successfully potty train their children. I have to start by thanking my oldest daughter, Elle, who started me on my path to becoming a potty-training expert. Without the challenges of potty training Elle, I would never have started to research potty training and help the thousands of moms around the world who have struggled with potty training. To my middle daughter, Saylor, thank you for teaching me how to successfully potty train a child who had been in and out of the hospital with heart surgeries and learning delays. I can't forget our youngest daughter, Scottie, one of those kids who picks up potty training in a day and doesn't look back—your spirit keeps me going and gives me hope. To my husband, Christopher, who always supports and encourages me to do better, think better, and be better, and never takes me too seriously. To my dear mom, who tells me never to stop pursuing my dreams and always says, "Go for it!" Finally, thank you to the entire staff at Children's Hospital Los Angeles, who continue to save and change lives on a daily basis, and to Dr. Andy Chang for supporting me in researching potty training.

About the Author

 **Megan Pierson, MA** is the founder of Potty Shop OC, a potty-training consultant, toddler sleep consultant, and author. Holding an MA in early childhood special education, Megan has a passion for helping children and their families lead happy and healthy lives.

Megan is the author of *Surviving and Thriving: Toddler Sleep Guide, Toddler Naps: Going from 2-1-ALL DONE, Yes, You Can! Potty Training Manual*, and coauthor of *Dear Mr. Covid*, a children's book.

Megan, her husband of 17 years, Christopher, and their three children reside in Orange County, California. Megan gives hope to all parents experiencing the "terrible twos" or a "threenager" and is your go-to gal when it comes to all things potty training.